PARADES
How to Plan, Promote & Stage Them

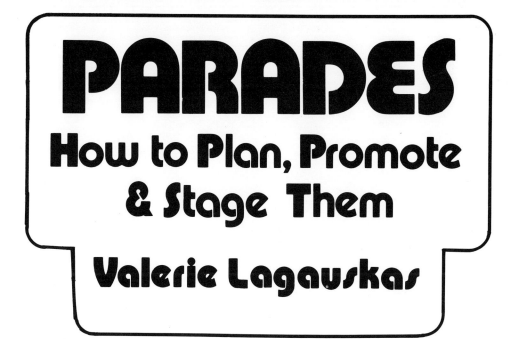

PARADES
How to Plan, Promote & Stage Them

Valerie Lagauskas

STERLING
PUBLISHING CO., INC. NEW YORK

The author and publisher would like to thank the following for the use of their photographs (numerals indicate page numbers): Anchorage Fur Rendezvous: 8, 24, 57, 80, 86, 112; Chamber of Commerce of Greater North Adams, Inc., North Adams, Massachusetts: 15; George A. DeBlois: 146; Detroit Renaissance Foundation/Robert Koyton, photographer: 148; Frankenmuth Chamber of Commerce, Frankenmuth, Michigan/Sue Beyer, photographer: 64, 76, 106, 110, 124; Graetz Bros., Ltd.: 31; Holland Tulip Time Festival, Inc., Holland, Michigan: 11, 107; Metro Dade County Department of Tourism. Miami, Florida: 25, 103, 108; Minneapolis Aquatennial Association: 12, 35, 72, 74, 82, 104, 133, 142; National Peanut Festival, Inc., Dothan, Alabama: color page D; NBC-TV: 78; John F. Ringwald: 111.

Library of Congress Cataloging in Publication Data

Lagauskas, Valerie.
  Parades: how to plan, promote & stage them.

  Includes index.
  1. Parades. I. Title.
GT3980.L33   791'.6   81-85038
ISBN 0-8069-0236-1   AACR2
ISBN 0-8069-0237-X (lib. bdg.)

Copyright © 1982 by Sterling Publishing Co., Inc.
Two Park Avenue, New York, N.Y. 10016
Distributed in Australia by Oak Tree Press Co., Ltd.
P.O. Box K514 Haymarket, Sydney 2000, N.S.W.
Distributed in the United Kingdom by Blandford Press
Link House, West Street, Poole, Dorset BH15 1LL, England
Distributed in Canada by Oak Tree Press Ltd.
% Canadian Manda Group, 215 Lakeshore Boulevard East
Toronto, Ontario M5A 3W9
Manufactured in the United States of America
All rights reserved

Contents

To my father

(*Opposite*) *Anchorage Fur Rendezvous special unit.*

Introduction

My association with parades began in 1963 when I was hired by Macy's as a secretary. My first appearance in the Macy's Parade was as Alice In Wonderland. From the date of my employment in January, all my desires, energies and thoughts were concentrated on holding out until the parade date in November. This was meant to be a temporary job to carry me until I went back to college the following fall semester.

As it turned out, nearly twenty parades later, it's still a little like Wonderland. I can assure you that regardless of the size of your event, if you produce a parade more than one year in a row it will always be exciting. It is always a new challenge because you never know what is going to happen. You can anticipate every possible pitfall, take care of all the loopholes, and just as you sit back and relax, something goes wrong.

My fifteenth parade was a prime example. We had marvelous cooperation from all our volunteers, the talent was all confirmed, no last-minute costume fittings were necessary, rehearsals had gone off without a hitch, the balloons had arrived safely from storage in Georgia, and the weather report was perfect.

I went into the production meeting with NBC with everything set and my sense of humor in fine form. Then, as we were sitting in Studio 8H at the NBC Studios in New York City's Rockefeller Center on the day prior to the parade, a small white light began flashing directly in front of me on the console. Being careful not to disturb any of the fifty or so others in the room, I picked up the telephone receiver.

On the other end was a voice from Hoboken, New Jersey. "The cars needed to pull the floats were delivered without registrations and the Port Authority says if we try to go through the Lincoln Tunnel the Thanksgiving Day Parade floats will be confiscated and the drivers arrested. . . . I think we have a problem."

My spontaneous answer to that broke up the meeting for a moment. I quickly excused myself, found an empty office and began making calls. One of my first calls was to the Port Authority police. I tried to convince them how terrible it would look if Thursday's papers announced that we had been forced to cancel the Thanksgiving Day Parade, including Santa Claus's appearance, because of the Port Authority of New York and New Jersey. Well, they weren't buying. I was told that the only person who could make an exception to their regulations was the Chairman, and "he doesn't believe in Santa Claus, anyway. Besides, he's en route to the Bahamas for the weekend."

Fortunately, after much hair-pulling and contact-calling, the problem was finally resolved with the aid of the New York City Police Department. Chief Dan Courtney, then Chief of the Manhattan South District, called in all the interested parties and was instrumental in finding a solution. The parade went on as scheduled. The drivers were not arrested, and Santa Claus arrived on the scene as planned.

New York's Finest annually lead Macy's Thanksgiving Day Parade.

My years at Macy's and of talking to festival directors from all around the country have taught me that the one constant "must" for a good parade is a close working relationship with the local police department. With their cooperation what could be major catastrophes are often routinely handled with a minimum of effort.

However, a good working relationship is a two-way street. You must be prepared to listen to their advice and to deal with the problems that your event is going to cause the police. This could be as simple as finding a place for the Police Chief's daughter on a float or as major as changing your whole parade route to avoid a hospital zone.

Being basically optimistic, I firmly believe there is no problem that cannot be solved. You may not always be enthusiastic about the solution but there's no point in getting sick over it. Learn what you can from the experience and jump back in.

Assuming you have been given the responsibility for staging a parade in your community, I'd like to offer some guidelines and an answer or two to help along the way.

Street scrubbing, in the Dutch tradition, precedes the parade in the Holland Tulip Time Festival, Holland, Michigan.

What and When Will It Be?

This, of course, may have already been decided for you. It could be the Fourth of July, the day the first crocus was seen in your state (a little chancy), or to commemorate some local hero on his birthday. The Sons of Norway celebrate their Constitution Day in this country with parades, banquets, and festivals. The *Syttende Mai* (May 17th) Celebration in Brooklyn this year includes about 5,000 people in the parade and another 70,000 watching. As with our July Fourth celebration, it is always definite when the event will take place. This particular section of Brooklyn claims to have the largest concentration of Norwegians outside of Norway. The event receives a great deal of municipal support, and the mayor of New York has been one of the honored guests.

Of course, an ethnic event may not be right for your community. It's only one idea. With some creative thought and energy you can come up with a project that will be entertaining and newsworthy—drawing attention to both the event and your

(Opposite) Minneapolis Aquatennial Association makes excellent use of its waterfront facilities.

community—and fun for those of you who will work so hard to make it happen.

Regional events are as varied as the many faces of our country. Cities on the water should capitalize on this asset, i.e.: the Parade of Tall Ships, Operation Sail (part of the bicentennial celebration in New York); Boston's 350th-birthday regatta; and the continuing parade of boats in Austin, Texas.

Somewhat different I'll grant you, but imagine a parade of skiers coming down the entire rugged length of a mountain at night, bearing torches. I'd recommend your participants all be experts here, but what a treat for the spectators!

Other areas offer different opportunities. Farming communities may wish to promote National Hog Week, or a local 4-H group may want to celebrate the triumphant completion of a project with a parade. In such a parade country livestock and equipment may play a heavy part in the festivities. Be creative. Be innovative. Be sensitive to your community and its needs, and you will be rewarded with public interest and continued success with your event.

Your decision when to hold your parade and its theme may be one and the same, but not necessarily so. Macy's Thanksgiving Day Parade has a continuing theme which is "entertainment for children." We sometimes stretch it a little to "children of all ages" when we include the Rockettes, Lionel Hampton, or Luciano Pavarotti. Eaton's in Montreal, on the other hand, does maintain a very strict children's-parade theme for their Christmas parade. The Pasadena Tournament of Roses, however, changes its theme each year. While each float is covered entirely in organic material, the designs vary considerably from year to year.

Whatever it may be, the selection of a theme is an important step, for it not only acts as a guideline for participants and planners alike, it also affords a promotional "hook" to inspire press and public interest in the activity.

Volunteer corps can fill a lineup, as in this Massachusetts parade.

2

God Bless
the Volunteers!

During my early years with Macy's, before I became actively involved in the actual operation of the parade, I marched as a butterfly or the Statue of Liberty or anything else they happened to need. It never occurred to me that anyone capable of walking would not want to be part of this spectacular event. Yet each Thanksgiving morning at the store while savoring my seven A.M. coffee and doughnut, after donning my costume, this announcement would come over the loudspeaker: "Anyone wishing to become a balloon handler, please report to the patio on the eighth floor. Those of you who are assigned to clown costumes may be given balloon lines at the parade assembly area."

As my responsibilities changed to include more of the parade operation, the magnitude of the event began to come into perspective. Each year, Macy's New York, a major retail organization, stages what began as a promotional event and has become a national institution. With the help of close to 2,500 volunteers, from stockboys to vice presidents, from the sales

(Opposite) Clowns not only involve the spectator, they have fun, too.

personnel to the maintenance department, Macy's employees all give of their time on Thanksgiving morning to make the day special for over 3 million people on the streets of New York and another 80 million viewers across the country.

Presently, a core group called the "Parade Committee," which numbers about twenty volunteers, works on the parade year-round. Each person has specific responsibilities related to a particular area of parade function. Meetings are held monthly with the whole group. Subgroups often meet on specific problem areas. One factor very common among those people who volunteer for the Parade Committee is that there is no time when two or more will meet, in the hall, in the street, or over a drink, without the parade being discussed.

This "rule by committee" was not always the case at Macy's. During my adolescence I worked at Macy's as secretary to S. Bernard Sklar. It was also at this time that I was becoming more interested in the workings of the parade. But as I was to learn, the operations were handled by a close handful of people and entry into this circle was privileged indeed.

Bernie at this time was Assistant to the Senior Vice President for Sales Promotion. As such, he rated an office the size of a small pantry. Its one redeeming feature was that it had what was probably the world's greatest view of the Empire State Building, through a window which literally took up half the wall.

Bernie is a hardworking man. It followed that in order to keep up, I often had to work late. One evening, in the middle of dictation, the door burst open and the Senior Vice President poked his head in. "Long time no see, Bernie! By the way, you've just been made Parade Director. See me tomorrow." And the door closed.

As the papers settled back down on the desk and the import

Giant pole puppet created especially for Macy's Parade.

Float escorts can bring the color and excitement of the float from the center of the street to the curb.

of what had been said set in, we kind of looked at each other and shrugged. Well, there I was. Not only was I going to be part of the privy group, I had to take notes at their meetings.

The parade had happened more or less on schedule for about 37 years by this time, but the spirit was slowly dying from neglect. Many people who had worked on the event for years—some from the very first—no longer felt a part of it. The most poorly attended party was the Parade Captains' dinner. The original purpose of this event was to thank those parade participants who contributed a good deal of the energy to make the show happen. These were the very people who avoided this evening's festivities.

What I learned about the care and nourishment of a volunteer labor force in those early years with Bernie was invaluable. The whole parade organization was examined in detail, and the number of long-term volunteers was astounding. Some people had actually been in the first parade in 1924. The core group was expanded to include many old parade hands. They finally received the recognition they deserved within the parade organization and became members of the Parade Committee.

VOLUNTEERS IN KEY POSTS

Whether your event is being staffed by volunteers from the community or a local organization, an important tip as valid to the Tournament of Roses Organization and to Macy's as to your event when electing officers or members to the committee or board, is to choose volunteers for key posts on the basis of past performances and interest—never, never on the basis of personal friendship or political influence. Only through the opportunity

Macy's Rollie Awards Dinner affords a break for volunteers and staff alike the week prior to the Thanksgiving Day Parade.

The Rollie is to Macy's what the Oscar is to the movie industry.

for advancement within your organization will you be assured of a loyal and enthusiastic group of volunteers. If they see the merit system can work for them, they will work harder for you and bring friends along.

Max Colwell of the Pasadena Tournament of Roses offers the following advice to parade organizers: "Employment of a manager or director of a community event is advantageous for the established festival and well-funded, large city organization. A manager will coordinate the work of volunteers, keep a sharp eye on the finances and make every effort to keep the unpaid work force enthused and happy."

He also goes on to offer some sound advice to the prospective director. "The lifeblood of a volunteer work force is in the recognition received, names in the newspaper, and credit for the success. Keep your volunteers out in front, on the speaking platform taking the bows, and in the news columns. You will then be rewarded with a loyal and enthusiastic membership."

In 1966, in order to demonstrate appreciation to all these persistent souls who had served Macy's Thanksgiving Day Parade unselfishly, the "Rollie" was born. The Rollie is a statue of a clown's head sculpted by Manfred Bass, designer and builder of Macy's Thanksgiving Day Parade floats. The name is a shortened form of Roland H. Macy, founder of Macy's. The Rollie is now to Macy's what the Oscar is to the motion-picture industry. Volunteers receive the Rollie just prior to their sixth parade after they have served at captain's rank or higher for five years.

The Rollie has become so coveted by parade volunteers that, in some cases when job assignments take them to outlying markets or even to other jobs with other companies, many people come back to complete that "one-more parade" to get their Rollie. And then there are those volunteers who left Macy's for other jobs, received a Rollie, and still keep coming back because of the team spirit and comradery.

COMMUNITY INVOLVEMENT

Millions of Americans do love a parade, and so do television networks, commercial sponsors, chambers of commerce, ethnic groups, and a potpourri of other organizations. They view parades not only as entertainment, but as demonstrations of community involvement and merchandising opportunities as well. Just consider the possibilities of the circus parade from train to tent and the department-store event. Imagine the marketing opportunities afforded by the chance to promote the climate of the Sun Coast of Florida or the benefits orange juice. Think of the ethnic pride after a parade about the virtues of Polish-Americans and their contributions to our society.

If your event is being produced by the community for the benefit of the community, then your volunteer structure will differ from that of a strictly commercial event. In many instances, a commercial event is of such benefit to a community that a great deal of municipal support is donated.

In Atlanta, the Women's Chamber of Commerce, in looking for an effective method to contribute to the economic and social betterment of Atlanta communities, produced its first Dogwood Festival, in 1968. Among its many goals, the organization wanted to gain recognition for Atlanta as a city concerned not only with economic growth but with esthetic values that make it a better place to live and work.

In order to achieve these goals, the Women's Chamber of Commerce of Atlanta established a Dogwood Festival organiza-

Orange Bowl fans will recognize this King Orange helium-filled balloon.

tion plan to ensure continuity of this event annually. Since the festival is a community event, many organizations lend support with volunteers and assume responsibility for different aspects of the festival and parade. They depend on the expertise of the Shriners to do the parade order and act as marshalls for the parade. A fraternity at Georgia Tech provides manpower for the parade as one of their projects, and they have a steering committee for the parade made up of many representatives of the business community.

Considered one of the best by festival and band communities, the St. Petersburg Festival of States in St. Petersburg, Florida, is a week-long event that includes both a Youth Parade and a Parade of States, as well as an Illuminated Night Parade. All are produced and run by the Suncoasters Organization. The Suncoasters and Herb Mellany, Managing Director of the Festival of States celebration, have made this event one of the South's largest civic celebrations.

The Suncoasters Organization is made up of St. Petersburg businessmen and professionals dedicated to producing the annual Festival of States celebration and related events. Sitting along the parade route in a beach chair you have brought along for the occasion, you may buy your program from the owner of a local bank, or the president of the Power and Light Company may offer to sell you a button to commemorate your visit to St. Petersburg.

Incentive for membership in this particular civic organization is a sincere desire to help the community and help build a better understanding among business and professional people, through their voluntary participation in an event of significant importance to the entire community. The members also demonstrate the success that can be achieved through cooperation between private enterprise and local government.

During my visit to the Festival of States in 1974, I received my first taste of true "Southern hospitality." My original purpose in visiting St. Petersburg was to view what I had heard was a truly fine band competition—fifteen bands representing the finest from as many states. I had long since learned the importance of marching bands to the success of a parade.

Representing Macy's Thanksgiving Day Parade, I was unprepared for the widespread community involvement demonstrated by the Suncoasters. Macy's runs a parade on Thanksgiving using volunteers, primarily Macy's employees. Community involvement is in the form of cooperation by major city agencies (police, fire, sanitation departments, etc.). I am sure that the success of such events as the Festival of States reflects directly upon the willingness of volunteers throughout the business community to undertake Festival assignments cheerfully and to carry them out thoroughly.

(*Opposite*) *Infantry from Fort Richardson in full arctic gear—including "bunny boots"—march in the Anchorage Fur Rendezvous.*

3 So We Have All These Volunteers, Now What?

As with any organization, be it corporation or parade, there should be one person at the top. Call this person Director, Manager, Grand Marshal, or Head Honcho, this is the puppeteer who will make the whole organization come to life and work together. The selection of this person should be carefully made, as the smoothness of the whole operation will be choreographed by him (or her). Developing an event over a period of months absolutely requires a smoothly run organization.

This person will have to know every aspect of parade operations, be able to relate well to the volunteer organization, and appreciate the kind of manpower available. In some cases, committee positions are filled by volunteers on a rotation basis. An assignment may be of two- or three-year duration and then a move is made to another area of responsibility. This very effectively builds a large pool of knowledgeable recruits and also stimulates their continued interest in the whole event. The director may be selected from this pool or may be someone hired specifically for the job.

(Opposite) Sometimes a good laugh can bring things into perspective.

A good director will come up with new ideas for enhancing an event and making it bigger and better each year. He should always be available to listen and learn. Guard against becoming a know-it-all. You will find it pays dividends to slip some of these great ideas to your president, or to one of your board members. Let him advance it as his own. It may be hard on your ego not to receive credit, but it will come later when the board members discuss the budget and decide that you are underpaid.

As stated earlier, a good director must supervise and motivate the volunteers. The volunteer force will have to be broken down into various committees, such as:

Executive Committee. This group, along with the director, handles all the day-to-day planning, financial, and operational activities of the parade organization, and coordinates the activities of the other committees.

Community Liaison Committee. This group works with city, county, and state officials, and seeks police, fire, and sanitation department cooperation.

Planning and Policy Committee. This group establishes criteria for total parade planning, from the theme and number of units in the parade to the length of the route.

Floats Committee. This includes coordination with sponsors regarding float design, construction, and selection.

Band Committee. This committee concerns itself with the selection of bands, invitations, housing, and everything else related to the bands in the parade.

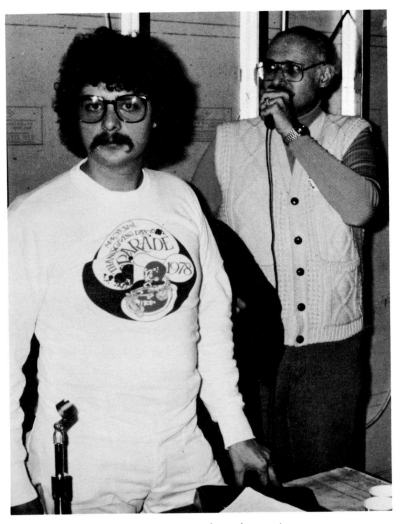

Volunteers can be involved in all aspects of parade operations.

Committee responsibilities should be clearly defined.

Other Units Committee. This could include selection of other units that will enhance your event (i.e.: clowns, antique cars, Scout groups, equestrian acts, etc.).

Manpower Committee. This group recruits volunteers as needed.

Programs-and-Such Committee. Programs, buttons, banners, T-shirts, and other memorabilia are great for raising funds. The development of this area is a very effective way to spread the word about your event and bring in some cash, too.

Publicity Committee. This committee sees to it that the community hears about and looks forward to your parade.

Ticket Committee. This is only necessary if you have grandstand seating (a good source of revenue).

Legal Matters and Insurance Committee: This committee examines possible difficulties, so major problems can be avoided.

Safety and Security Committee. This committee may act as liaison with local police, emergency, and hospital organizations.

Parade Lineup Committee. This group determines the order of things.

Starting-Line Committee. The people on this committee control the assembly-area operations.

Marshalling Committee. This committee deals with the movement of the parade on the street.

Communications Committee. This is the group that tells the back of the parade what the front is doing.

Dispersal Committee. This group ensures smooth breakup of the parade at the end of the line of march.

The above are just some suggested areas for committee development. Your particular parade organization will depend on the size of your event and how you want it structured. In any case, a good volunteer staff is essential to a large parade.

Also, whether it's done by a volunteer committee or by a person hired specifically for the function, publicity is absolutely a must for any group planning an event. After all, why bother, if no one knows about it? Good publicity can take a small local event like the Pasadena Tournament Parade and snowball it into one of the top promotional events in the country. Publicity, along with a good marketing plan, can spell success for your event.

In Toronto, Eaton's audience eagerly awaits the Santa Claus Parade.

Major festivals like a World's Fair can spark innovative ideas.

Timetable

Time is a very important planning ingredient in any parade. Planning time, time of the parade, and length of performance all make a difference. Decide early in your planning how much time you want your parade to take passing any given point on your line of march. The Tournament of Roses Parade takes two hours to pass a location along its five-and-a-half-mile route. Of course, you can just keep adding elements to your event and then determine how long it will be. But if you're the type who can't say no, you may end up with a 1,000 unit parade, taking six hours to pass a point on your ten-mile course.

Limiting the time of your show also limits the number of elements it can comfortably contain. Research has provided some pretty basic guidelines here. Generally a 100-unit parade will fit into a two-hour time frame. Recommended speed varies from two miles per hour to three miles per hour, with approximately 100-foot intervals between units.

(Opposite) This float carries racing cars as well as a television star. Telecast time will affect the parade timetable.

Often parade managers control the speed of their show by having every unit conscious of the speed limit. I've found in many cases it is just as effective—and in some cases more so—to have only your lead units control their speed. Everything that follows is then instructed to allow 100 feet between it and the element in front. This can keep a parade from becoming an accordion if a problem occurs.

Long gaps in a parade are boring to spectators. Remember, when you put your show on the road, it's *your* audience out there. Please them and you will be rewarded with growing enthusiasm for your parade. Displease them, and you'll hear about it, particularly when you try to get a permit to stage your event the next year. Often your audience will be sitting on the curb or in lawn chairs hours before the start of the parade. It's all part of the festivities. Community members and their friends and family will all be waiting for neighbors, community dignitaries, and special guests to pass by.

Causes for gaps in parades are as varied as the elements themselves: A float may have a flat tire; a group of clowns may stop to include some of the audience in their antics; a band may

Cherry Festival spectators improvise grandstands.

Friday, July 17
Summer Break Kick Off Ceremonies, TCF Atrium
Junior Tennis Tourney – U of M Courts
Nicollet Mall "Summer Break" Block Party
Youth & Senior Art Display, Marquette Bank

Saturday, July 18
Legislator's Day, Downtown
Grande Day Parade, Parade Stadium
Aqua Brass Drum & Bugle Comp., Parade
    Stadium
Aquatennial Celebrity Regatta, Lake Calhoun
Sky of 10,000 Frisbees Tournament,
    Ft. Snelling State Park
Aqua Windsurfing Exhibition, Lake Calhoun

Sunday, July 19
Milk Carton Boat Races, Lake Calhoun
Water Ski Show of Stars, Lake of the Isles

Monday, July 20
Suburban Queen's Review Luncheon
Senior "Summer Break '81", Government Ctr.
International Entertainment, NSP Plaza

Tuesday, July 21
Downtown Queens Review Luncheon
Senior "Summer Break '81", Government Ctr.

Wednesday, July 22
Mayor's Day, Downtown
8-Mile Race, Parade Route
Torchlight Parade, Parade Stadium

Thursday, July 23
Queen's Flight in Fashion, Apache Plaza
Nicollet Mall Art Fair
Plaza and Shopping Center Shows Daily

Friday, July 24
Queen of the Lakes Coronation,
    Children's Theatre
Nicollet Mall Art Fair
Hot Air Balloons, Burnsville Ctr.

Saturday, July 25
Bike Races, Lake Harriet
Flotilla Frolic, Mississippi River
Aqua-Oly "100", Elko Speedway

Sunday, July 26
Youth & Family Expo, Loring Park
Pepsi Powerboat Challenge, Lake Calhoun
Youth Day Parade, Loring Park
Fireworks Finale, Lake Calhoun

Complete Program and Ticketing Information:
Program Director
Minneapolis Aquatennial Association
702 Wayzata Blvd., Commodore Court
Minneapolis, MN 55403
Tel: (612) 377-4621
Over 250 programmed events featuring the
cultural and entertainment contributions of
Finland, Taiwan, Australia, and renowned
American groups.

The Minneapolis Aquatennial includes many activities other than parades.

do a little counter-marching or a Shrine group may do a little extra maneuver for some special friends in the grandstands; a politician may step out of the parade to shake hands. Many of these potential problems can be anticipated in your ground rules to marchers. (A sample of these appears on page 151.) Others can be resolved by your marshalling procedures on the spot.

Most important, if you plan to start your parade at 9 A.M., do so. All your parade units, marchers, and riders should be in position at least fifteen minutes—and preferably thirty—before you open the show. Key committee personnel should be asked to report even earlier so that you can make adjustments if anyone is ill. Your assembly area should be thoroughly checked by your committee to ensure all is in readiness. Decisions on how to deal with late arrivals should be made in advance of parade day and enforced. You may elect to group all late arrivals at the end of the parade, fit them in when they arrive, or leave them out altogether.

One year, Macy's decided to use a particular marching band for the opening of the show. However, when the group found out that they would not be marching, they were very disappointed. So we arranged to have their buses waiting as they finished the opening portion of the show at the store. Police escort—lights flashing and sirens blaring—brought them up to 77th Street.

The only problem was that the unit they were supposed to follow, Bullwinkle the Moose, had left the starting line ten minutes before and the last float, Santa Claus, was just leaving when they arrived. I'll always remember their short, chubby band director as I passed him and the band running through the parade line of march to their position about one mile away. He was shaking his head, saying, "Never again! Never again!"

Ahh! The wonderfulness of marching bands.

ADVANCE PLANNING

Occasionally, potential parade managers have visited my office looking for some direction in putting together parades. When I've asked when they were planning to hold their events, the answers have varied from three years to six weeks.

Advance planning for the Macy's Parade is a must, in part because of the NBC Network telecast which treats it as a live spectacular stage show. As such, there are many requirements and problems which ordinarily would not affect a parade.

Macy's Thanksgiving Day Parade actually stops so that each unit is given a chance to perform for the cameras. At this writing, no other parade in the country is staged this way on national television. This has lead to some problems. Broadcasting a live television show from a studio is chancy enough, but take cameras, lights, crew, and action out onto the street in November in New York City and anything can happen—and has.

Since the televised show is timed second by second, we schedule the arrival of the parade at the staging area in front of the store so that we have about a ten-minute buffer. This time is planned as a safeguard against breakdowns and any other problems that could delay the parade from being in position at 35th Street and Broadway when the clock strikes 10:00 A.M. and the whole country expects the New York City Mounted Police to usher Macy's Thanksgiving Day Parade into Herald Square.

You'd think we would have this down pat, right? Wrong!

About seven years ago, the Police Department informed us that, because of their new schedule, the police who assist in holding back the crowds along the line of march would not report until one half hour later than in the past. This meant, of course, that the parade could not start until 9:30 A.M. at 77th

Street and Central Park West, a full two-and-a-half miles north of the telecast area. What were we to do? Short of putting everyone on roller skates to get them downtown in less than thirty minutes, we had to come up with a plan to start the show on time and still comply with the police request to leave later. Our solution has never been admitted in print before.

We actually staged the first ten minutes of the show as a mini-parade downtown, complete with mounted escort, band, float, and clowns. The only difference was that these elements were not seen by the over two million people who lined the parade route, but the show started on time on NBC, and hardly anyone was the wiser—we hope. Fortunately, the Police Department changed their schedule after only a few years, and we now leave 77th Street at 9:00 A.M., giving our lead marshalls plenty of time to arrive.

During those few years, however, we did have some interesting moments. One particular cold, rainy Thanksgiving morning, I remember getting a frantic call at 8:00 A.M. at 77th Street. "The Doodlebug's not here," shouted a concerned Macy's senior executive, who was handling the downtown street operation. A moment of panic ensued. It was pretty hard to misplace the Doodlebug, as it was about 10 feet high, 150 feet long, was green all over and had long, glitzy eyelashes. Relative calm returned when a look at the operations plan determined that the 'bug had been safely nestled in Macy's sub-sub basement for two days and was not due out on the street until 8:30 A.M.

Since Macy's Thanksgiving Day Parade has been around for over fifty years, we often find we are working a year or two in advance, particularly where bands and floats are concerned. If your event develops into the luxury of an annual event, I'm sure you'll find your own lead-time schedule becoming more roomy.

The following pictures are a selection from Macy's Thanksgiving Day Archives. Storybook characters are often used in float designs.

Copying can be effective but make sure you get permission before getting too literal.

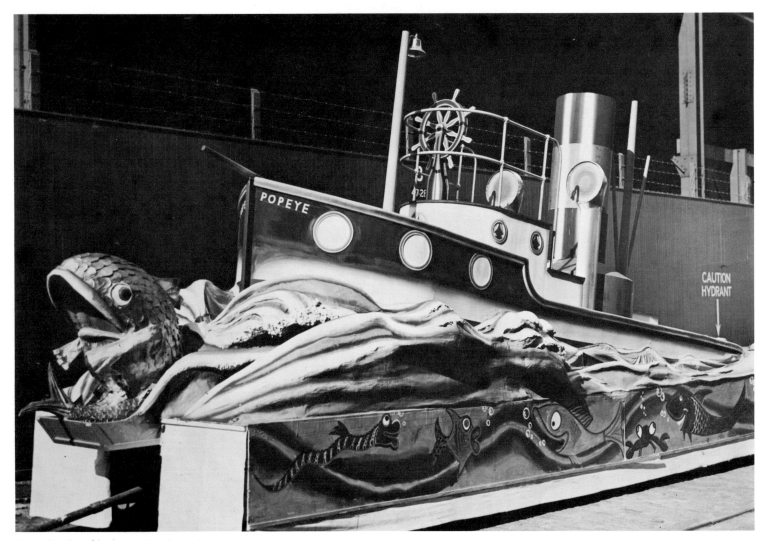

Popeye has long been a popular float subject.

Clown heads turn ordinary people into gigantic puppets.

Pinocchio was a balloon character in an early Macy's Parade.

Both Pinocchio and Ferdinand the Bull patiently wait to join the parade.

This float depicts a very basic structure.

Basic structure can be enhanced by the addition of superstructures and sculpted figures.

Early Macy's Parades were telecast as news events.

Commentators build anticipation by describing forthcoming parade elements.

In this early float, Gulliver seems quite tied up.

Pull-float and appropriately costumed escorts are flexible parade units.

This early Macy's Parade passes through Columbus Circle on its way to Herald Square.

Fantasy characters continue down the line of march.

This Cowardly Lion pull-unit saw many Macy's Parades.

Times Square on Thanksgiving Day.

Planning the Show

Before dealing deeply with parade-day problems, think about the types of possible elements that can make up a parade:

Floats
Bands
Balloons
Clowns and novelty acts
Honor guards
Vintage autos
Fire Department
Police Department

Equestrian groups
Unicyclists, bicyclists, tricyclists
Celebrities
Festival queens
Visiting royalty
A herd of prize 4-H sheep
Military
Talent acts

You must decide what types of entries you want in your event. A local volunteer fire association parade contains drill teams, bands and drum corps, comedy teams, and fire companies, departments, or auxiliaries. Of course, this type of event offers the surrounding communities the opportunity to show off their

(Opposite) *Production meetings become more concentrated as the parade nears.*

equipment, marching skills, and style. The Tournament of Roses Parade includes only floats, bands, and equestrian units. Macy's Thanksgiving Day Parade includes floats, balloons, bands, clowns, an occasional equestrian unit, and antique celebrity cars.

A key factor in planning your show is balance. You shouldn't have floats of similar size, shape, and color near each other. Also, bands of similar styles should be separated. (Then again, you may want the kilted bands grouped and the Savings and Loan Association floats in the front of the parade.)

The lead elements of your parade should be sufficiently exciting to open the show with splash. A large, exciting band, an animated colorful float, perhaps police motorcycles or horses and **official cars may** lead off your show. Remember, when you've created this initial impact, don't let the rest of the parade fall flat. Space your elements to create a series of high moments. Separating bands will allow you to highlight a corps-style group and, after a few other units go by, a Highland band can lend a whole new excitement.

Needless to say, no matter how you perceive your show, you must become thoroughly familiar with each element when you accept the entry. The auxiliary fire department from the next town may send a contingent to march, but they may also send their oldest and newest equipment for display, as well as a team of trained dalmatians. You should know this in advance. You will not relish surprises on the morning of your event.

A variety of marching units helps to create balance.

Mr. Chuck, Macy's official clown, riding the self-propelled Cootie float in the Macy's Thanksgiving Day Parade.

The Rockettes perform annually on Broadway in front of Macy's for the NBC telecast of the parade.

Specially designed cranberry gnome costumes complement an Ocean Spray float.

The Doodlebug, 150 feet long, undulates through Herald Square. There is a garden tractor in its head, and it has animated eyes and glitzy eyelashes.

Kingsley Fourth Grade Symphonette Band performs in the Cherry Festival Junior Parade in Traverse City, Michigan.

Grand lady with caveman in tow.

Group of children in American Indian costumes. Each element was numbered, corresponding to the position in the assembly area and parade.

Parade entries can be as simple and timely as this baseball fan during the strike.

Band competition affords an opportunity for greater band exposure.

In Traverse City, marching bands lend excitement to the parade. →

1976 Operation Sail used the Hudson River for its line of march during the Bicentennial.

In Yorktown, New York, a fife-and-drum group offers a more formal parade presentation during the July Fourth presentation. →

(Below left) Corporate-sponsored floats add variety to parades. This is an example of simple float construction.

(Below right) The vehicle pulling this float is disguised as part of the overall theme. Driver visibility is somewhat restricted.

Macy's giant Kermit the Frog balloon was on display in Hyde Park, London, at a special celebration for the International Year of the Child, sponsored by the Queen. ←

A nighttime parade. The Illuminated Parade, in St. Petersburg, Florida. Lighting captures the excitement of the imaginative float entry for the Maas Brothers. →

Dothan, Alabama, National Peanut Festival. As a highlight of this parade, a cement mixer filled with peanuts pours them out, to the delight of the spectators. →

Special lift equipment was used in setting up the balloon and later to make any necessary repairs.

When possible, you should visit the bands you have accepted, study the plans for the float designs, and meet with the other entrants in the parade. "You" may be various committees, or individuals designated to follow up on certain areas of responsibility. The manager must, however, be fully apprised by these committees. In some cases it will benefit the event to have the manager follow through—perhaps by visiting school bands from outside the community. This may enhance the event in the schools' eyes, and bring additional attention to your community.

DETERMINING THE MARCHING ORDER

When you've decided what will be included in the parade, you have to determine an order. My own method for making sense out of chaos, is to write the name of each element on an index card, being careful not to leave any out. I color code the various groups, i.e., blue cards for bands, red ones for floats, green ones for clowns, etc. When this is completed, I take one group of cards at a time and place them either on the floor or on a large table.

The balloons in the Macy's Thanksgiving Day Parade are the hallmark of the event. There are usually eight or nine in a given year. I take my nine purple balloon cards and position them widely apart. Maybe one year Mickey Mouse will be the first balloon—the kids will love that! I try to position a new balloon late in the show. In 1980, Macy's unveiled its new Superman balloon, all 104 gorgeous feet of him. Okay, I've now started with Mickey Mouse, and Superman will bring up the rear.

Since the parade is telecast on NBC as a three-hour-long spectacular, I tend to think in terms of half-hour segments. The

Numbering each parade unit helps to organize the show. Star, the Caribou, has been a regular parade entrant in the Anchorage Fur Rendezvous for over fifteen years.

Each parade unit is written on individual index cards and then positioned.

first hour, the parade is shown as a moving parade as it leaves the assembly area. The last two hours are a stage show at Herald Square. All units in the parade are positioned as they will appear for the cameras. About 11:00 A.M. is considered the halfway mark of the stage show. Let's put Kermit the Frog here to excite the kids some more. All the rest of the balloons are positioned between Mickey and Kermit and Superman.

Now, to position the floats. Of course, Santa brings up the rear, but Macy's likes to alternate the Big Apple and the Turkey as the lead float. Again, consideration is given to the type of float, whether it's sponsored and the kind of performance planned on it. If more than one film is represented, they are not positioned in the same portion of the show. Likewise, if elements are compatible, I plan them together. The Kermit balloon and the Muppet Movie Bus are a good example of this. Also, I will place a Highland band near our Loch Ness float. Pretty soon, a pattern emerges—band, float, balloon, clowns, band, float, mounted drill team, balloon.

Never, never have a band follow a band in your parade. The results are terrible. Neither the bands nor the parade will benefit from the confusion of sounds—and especially not the audience. Place at least two units between bands. Be careful, though, not to have too quiet an event. Music is a wonderful addition to a parade and should be planned for. Floats can also benefit by having a sound system on board. Again, be sure to inform float sponsors of the level of sound you expect.

Once you have your index cards and are happy with the order, pin them up on the wall. Be sure to put in a lead car and cleanup units at the end. Study your order. Have it typed. Get to know it by heart. Leave your cards on the wall for quick, easy reference. The most up-to-date version of the lineup should be on the wall. Lineups change. Copies get made. Sometimes a secretary or volunteer may not dispose of all the earlier copies. Your lineup on the wall will serve as a guide.

Now the parade is a visible reality. You'll have to break it up into divisions. This will enable you to assign a marshall to each division. His responsibility is to field any problems and report any mishaps in the division during the parade. The easiest way is to have one marshall for every twelve or thirteen units—assuming you're still working with a 100-unit event.

If, based on the format of your parade, it will be difficult for one marshall to handle twelve or so units, then you should explore another method of control. Instead of having your marshalls move along with the parade, you can station them at every intersection along the route. In this manner they will be responsible for each unit as it passes through a specific area.

The Tournament of Roses Parade uses both types of marshalls. A marshall is assigned to each float. It is his responsibility to become thoroughly familiar with that particular float so he can field any problems that may arise. The marshall also accompanies the float throughout the entire parade. Marshalls are assigned to specific intervals along the route, as well.

THE MACY'S METHOD

Macy's Thanksgiving Day Parade, on the other hand, assigns a captain to each unit in the parade—band, float, balloon, clown, or specialty act. The parade is also broken down into sections and marshalls assigned accordingly. Each of the two division marshalls is responsible for half the parade. They must move up and down the parade through their section, troubleshooting.

The movie "The Wiz" was depicted in Macy's Parade by a float designed by artist Tony Walton.

Reporting to them, and each responsible for one quarter of the parade, are the assistant division marshalls. These may also travel through their portion of the show. Often, however, an assistant division marshall will be assigned to cover one particular trouble area along the route, either at Columbus Circle or in the Times Square area.

Next in the Macy's Parade are the unit marshalls, each responsible for one eighth of the parade. Captains for each element go to their respective unit marshalls in case of a problem. One reason why we have developed the "captain per element" method, has been to make Macy's Thanksgiving Day Parade run as smoothly as possible. The best way to accomplish this is through a good network of communications. Therefore, if a problem occurs, it can be quickly and efficiently resolved.

All of the marching bands in Macy's Parade, whether they come from New Jersey or Hawaii, are assigned captains who are their liaisons for the parade. The captain greets the band director, gets to know the person who actually controls the band on the street, then acts as advisor during the parade itself. The captain informs the director from whom he should get instructions at any point along the line, i.e.: If the band needs to slow up or march faster to maintain the one-hundred-foot gap after the preceding element.

Also, each clown group has its own captain. Of course, once in clown make-up, many of the recruits become anonymous. With over 600 clowns in the parade, our captains have their hands full. One year, at the parade assembly area, as the first units were preparing to step off, I was asked to make an announcement from my position on the sound truck. As it was my first general statement, I prefaced it with, "Good morning, everyone. Happy Thanksgiving." You can imagine my reaction

Last minute costume adjustments prior to Eaton's Santa Claus Parade.

61

when my family reported having heard me greet the crowd over a local radio station, only to follow it with, "Will all you clowns assemble on the sidewalk."

Each of the floats in Macy's Parade also has a captain. However, unlike the Tournament of Roses marshall, our captains do not require technical knowledge of the operation of the units. The float captains' responsibilities begin long before the parade itself. They are asked to recruit the people who will escort the float in costume. Float escorts are used to carry the excitement and color of the float right to each curb. After recruiting the escorts, a captain must arrange fitting schedules with the costume coordinator and plan a choreography session with the whole group.

On Thanksgiving Day, the captain assembles the escorts for a final briefing and session with the choreographer and meets the float driver. The driver will take all direction from the captain who will set the pace along the route.

My first parade assignment was float escort. I was assigned to the Storybook Float and costumed as Alice In Wonderland. The float was positioned just behind a band from Florida. The Mad Hatter and I did the Mexican Hat Dance all the way to Macy's. It's been many years since that first for me, but the thrill of seeing all the smiling—sometimes cold—faces responding to the parade, cannot be described. Be it laughing at clowns or booing at the bad guys, it's hard not to be responsive, regardless of your age.

Just remember that a parade is a very flexible event. Rules should be established, but experience may point to changes, and recurring problems may be an indication that a re-evaluation is in order. The first parade is always the most difficult. As with anything else, you must get off the ground before you can fly.

Thereafter, you learn more each year from your mistakes—and they will happen. There is no formula for staging a parade that will work everywhere for everybody. The variables are as many as there are people. The one rule which will get you through it **all** is "be as flexible as your event."

Macy's Float Captain.

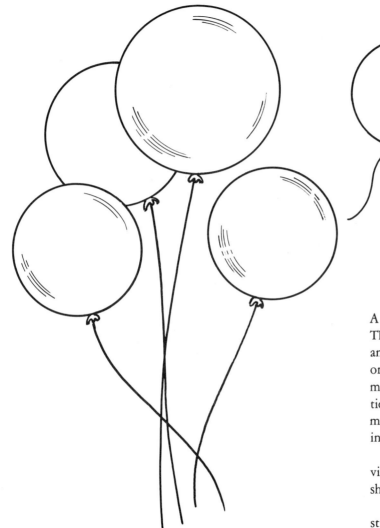

Parade Route

A great deal of thought should be given to selecting your route. The point at which the whole parade assembles should have ample street space for all the parts. A park area, school grounds, or piece of municipal property is often quite acceptable. Bands, marchers, and other participants will appreciate rest-room facilities both at the start and the end of the line of march. Provisions must be made also for school-bus parking, unloading and loading of horses, and dressing facilities for costumed characters.

Involve your local fire department and other emergency services to ensure proper access for fire and ambulance vehicles, should they prove necessary.

Locate a map of your city. Pay attention to overhead obstructions, excavations and construction, odd turns, or narrowing of pavement. When you have located a possible route, ask yourself the following questions:

(Opposite) Ethnic parades like the Frankenmuth, Michigan, Willkommen Bavarian Festival can exhibit community pride.

1. Is there room for assembly of elements at the beginning?

2. Does this route offer plenty of viewing area for spectators?

3. Are turns easily negotiable?

4. Are there any overpasses to be avoided?

5. Is there major construction under way?

6. Does this route avoid steep grades?

7. Are grandstand locations available?

8. Where will judging platforms be located?

9. Will there be a plentiful dispersal area at end of the route?

A good rule of thumb on length of the route is to have it exceed the actual length of the parade by at least one half a mile. This means that the front of your parade will reach the dismantling area after the last element has left the starting line. You can get some rough calculations by assuming the average element takes up fifty feet of space. If you maintain a 100-foot distance between units in a 100-unit parade, you get roughly 15,000 feet of parade, or approximately three miles. There is no law stating that this is the way it has to be, however. If your particular community wishes to hold a parade one and one half miles in length, this same 100-unit event will be accommodated as well. It just

Animal power is a very popular parade element.

means that later units will still be entering the line of march after the first divisions have crossed the finish line.

After the route has been finalized, drawings should be made of the entire route, the assembly area, and the dispersal area. Each element in the parade should be positioned on these maps according to your lineup.

Once these maps are finalized, they should be distributed to all parade and city officials, police and emergency services personnel, and parade participants. On the map for the line of march you should indicate positions of emergency tow vehicles and location of Red Cross ambulances. Location of viewing stands should also be noted, as well as any television camera locations. The more comprehensive the information, the less occasion for confusion.

The line of march should be clearly defined on the street as well. Perhaps you may elect to decorate the route or merely to close off intersections with barricades. Whatever you do, make sure there can be no question in the mind of visiting participants in your parade, which direction to march in. Your publicity person can be a great asset by arranging for the local newspapers to print the route as a public service. If this is done well, you can use the rows of happy faces to guide you along.

THE ASSEMBLY AREA

The space available for assembly will, of course, determine the method of formation. If you have a large park area, ball field or boulevard, it may be possible to form up there, so that all the elements are in position and need only to be called to step into the parade. In most instances, side streets will be used, and ele-

ments will move up and fall into the line of march when called. The assembly area should be set up with:

1. Sufficient space to line up all the float units in order of appearance;

2. Space for the bands to form up;

3. Clown formation area where props may be held;

4. Sufficient space for other elements to be grouped.

The assembly location is a key area of attention for me on Thanksgiving Day. We have a sound system set up to enable each area to hear the progress of the parade. From my vantage point on top of the sound truck, I get to oversee the whole assembly operation.

In addition to the over 2,000 Macy's employees, the bands, the performers, the police and the television crews, there is a whole group of spectators who position themselves just over the ready line to cheer each unit as it starts its parade journey. They applaud as enthusiastically for Big Bird as for a bunch of roller-skating clowns. And the greeting they give to out-of-town bands, makes them all feel welcome. Each balloon receives tremendous moral support as the handlers negotiate the turn onto Central Park West.

As I was climbing down from my position on the sound truck one particularly cold Thanksgiving morning, a man rushed over to me and began pumping my hand. He had moved into a new apartment several months before, not realizing that his bedroom windows would be witness to the spectacle of the

Bullwinkle rests prior to his parade appearance.

Eaton's floats are shipped via truck from warehouse to parade site.

Macy's Parade. He'd gone to bed early the night before, taking some medication for a cold he felt was coming on. (Remember now, he's telling me all this as I'm climbing over a railing, down the side of a truck, juggling my clipboard, and trying not to lose my derby hat.) About 7:30 A.M., he woke up feeling stuffy and was about to take a pill, when he glanced out the window and saw Bullwinkle peering in at him.

Hoping to get away quickly, I apologized if the noise of the parade disturbed him, and told him I hoped he would feel better soon.

"But you don't understand," he said. "I'm fine, just fine. At first I thought I was hallucinating, but it's all real. My cold is gone, and it's a wonderful day! Thank you! Thanks, Macy's!"

And it was a wonderful day!

THE FINISH LINE

As with any show, once the curtain comes down, the activity is only beginning for many backstage personnel. In a parade, the curtain comes down as each element passes the finish line. This area is as important as any in staging a parade.

Each element must know exactly where to go once it has finished the route. Any uncertainty can cause the whole parade to back up. The same effect would be achieved if you paid the toll on a crowded highway and, rather than proceeding, you stopped dead. Imagine the congestion. Now, imagine how all the creative energy you put into your show would be affected. Planning the dispersal area should include sufficient space to move elements away quickly, and space for dismantling floats, and loading horses and band buses.

Costumes can be created at home or by a professional costume house.

Another consideration is the dressing area for participants. Quite frequently, you can plan your event in such a way that all personnel will report in costume. This works well if your float units come from a nearby community or if your clowns each prepare their own costume and makeup. Much like other Broadway shows, however, Macy's Thanksgiving Day Parade provides costumes for all the clowns, float escorts, and balloon handlers as well as the parade officials. All personnel change into costumes at the store. We then bus them to the parade assembly area. The line of march returns to the Macy's at 34th Street and 7th Avenue. All the participants then change back to street clothes before leaving the area.

A smaller community may find it advantageous to stage a parade with a circular route. This works particularly well in areas where space is at a premium, because the assembly area can then serve as the dispersal area. Of course, the route must be long enough to allow the last units to clear before the first return. Just to avoid confusion, it is advisable to position a "traffic officer" at the end of the parade whose responsibility is limited to directing the various parade units to their respective dispersal areas.

Bringing up the rear of Macy's Parade are the huge street sweepers of the New York City Department of Sanitation. Largely ignored by the crowds, these unsung heros follow the Santa Float the entire distance of the parade route. Like washing the dishes after a meal, cleanup is a necessary part of community life. Crews of volunteer personnel are also assigned to the assembly and dispersal areas to see that parade-related litter is removed.

Again, cooperation with all city agencies ensures a successful event. It is best to explore all city requirements well before parade day. Volunteer assignments can assist where necessary, and complaints from neighbors can be avoided.

Band auxiliaries await their parade call.

Marching Bands

As far as I'm concerned, music is to a parade what thread is to a string of pearls. Silent marching groups, of course, have their place in a parade, but if the whole event is made up of row upon row of silent marchers, odds are it will get pretty boring for spectators. Musical units can include high school or college marching bands, drum-and-bugle corps, military bands, Mummers groups, and ethnic bands. School band programs offer a wonderful opportunity for young people to expand their artistic awareness, while developing discipline.

The parade committee should determine early in the planning stages of an event just what the musical emphasis will be. Philadelphia holds a Mummers Parade in celebration of each new year. The Portland Rose Festival invites outstanding marching bands from all over the country to participate in the parade and competition, held in Oregon each June.

Thought should be given to the type of bands to be included in your parade. If your parade date has been set, check the

(Opposite) Marching bands add the excitement of music to a parade.

A musical thread keeps your show together.

calendar to see if local schools are having exams that week, or football playoffs. These factors will certainly affect the availability of high school bands for your event. If you are interested in including drum-and-bugle-corps groups, be sure to check their competition schedules.

Once the date is settled and the availability of the groups is determined, one more decision should be made before sending out your invitations. Are you in a position to offset any of the costs related to the bands' transportation to your community? The parade committee may feel that a token amount can be donated to a school's "band fund" or to a drum corps' "travel budget." Include this informatioin in the invitation.

If the committee feels that such a contribution would seriously strain the parade budget, then this information must be part of your initial correspondence. In many cases a school will provide busing to nearby communities to enable the band to participate in events on a regular basis. Such participation offers an opportunity and a challenge to the students to play in public **and** is considered part of their education.

Send invitations well ahead of the date of your event and include a deadline for reply. The band committee may opt to invite all the high school bands within a 100-mile radius. The number of high school bands within this area may far exceed the number you feel you can safely include in your event. The invitation should then include the information that only the first fifteen or twenty to reply will be considered. This will also serve to encourage prospective band directors to get their replies in early.

BAND COMPETITIONS

Often, a successful response to parade invitations will prompt a local community to expand on the parade format to include a marching-band competition as a climax to the day's activities. Prizes can be either trophies and/or money. As the stature of the event grows, you'll find that bands will soon be asking to participate.

A band competition can do much to enhance an event. It must be handled properly. A regional judging association should be called in to work with you to develop the rules, and to adjudicate. The band committee may elect to make awards both for the competition and for the parade itself.

A band competition is also a good source of revenue and can help defray much of the parade's operating expenses. You'll require a stadium or school ballfield large enough for the drill performances to be appreciated. The high school in your community may be persuaded to play host to this event, its own marching band providing an exhibition for the visiting groups.

By bringing in bands for a competition, you'll find that you are also hosting the band members' parents, and other schoolmates, and friends. Each visitor represents another ticket sold and another program purchased. This may sound mercenary, but as long as your event maintains its standards of performance, these funds will enable it to grow in keeping with its reputation.

Like any performers, musicians like to be appreciated. Nothing can strengthen a band's performance and create a desire for quality musical education more than enthusiastic audience response. Each time a band travels outside its own district it takes with it the desire to associate with other quality musical units, learning and sharing ideas with other music directors and students. But not to be forgotten, a marching band takes with it the encouragement and recognition of hometown supporters. The desire to show what they can do inspires a band to accept the discipline necessary to excel.

The St. Petersburg Festival of States is a fine example of the value of effective development of a visiting-band program. In the description of the Festival of States as a band trip, band directors are informed of the basic philosophy. The success of this band program demonstrates its truth.

1. We will accept only one musical unit per state per year. There is no honor whatsoever in attending a festival where any group can get invited.

2. We are not doing any favors by "allowing" you to bring your band to our city. You are doing them for us. We realize this fact!

3. Musicians like to be appreciated for their endeavors. It is our responsibility to provide an alert, enthusiastic, and appreciative audience for your performances.

4. Since you are the stars of the show, you should be brought to the center of action. . . .

5. Your VIP's will receive extra hosting befitting their stature and position.

6. You will be treated by us exactly as we would want to be treated on a visit to your hometown.

SELECTING BANDS

A competition may not fit into your plans at this time. In all likelihood, though, bands and music will play an important part in your parade. Each year Macy's includes only a dozen or so bands in its parade lineup. These groups are selected from over 300 applications received annually. Each applicant is asked to submit a videotape or film of the band showing a drill performance, a record or tape of the group playing in concert, and a color photo of everyone in uniform.

Prospective musicians watch the show.

We also request background information on the band, competitions entered, awards won, and a biography of the band director. If a particular school district or state does not encourage competition, then we ask for information about festivals, exhibitions, or parades which the band has attended. Many fine bands are not permitted to compete because of local community or school-board restrictions, and we try to be as objective as possible in reviewing the materials submitted to us.

Over the years, Macy's has established a network of communication with festival directors and judges all over the country. This network has enabled us to call Traverse City, Michigan, or Disneyland, California, to get information about a particular group. Communication of this sort is a very good source of information and direction.

Another invaluable source of information is the International Festivals Association, based in Minneapolis. Not only are they in contact with the major festivals in the United States, Canada, and Mexico, but the I.F.A. also provides other festival-related information. Are you looking for a float builder in the Southwest, or a pipeline to band-travel experts? Your membership in the International Festivals Association entitles you to share information and experience with other members.

School bands enjoy an opportunity to take home a remembrance of a successful trip. A special flag, plaque, or certificate with the name of the event and date will be displayed proudly either at the school or, with flags, carried in other parades. Plan to make the presentation at a school assembly prior to or shortly after your event.

Also, depending upon the weather, band members will appreciate the availability of soft drinks or hot chocolate at the end of their march. This bit of hospitality should be extended if possible.

Bands can either be professional or amateur.

All the bands in Macy's Parade are visited prior to Parade Day by a Macy's representative and Dick Schneider, the Producer/Director of the NBC telecast. This is a very important step in the planning of a live television show. Each band's on-camera performance is reviewed and timed, and the camera cues noted. All the bands are told to prepare a two-minute drill performance for the telecast. Occasionally, when we've visited a school band, their performance during rehearsal has exceeded the time limit. We must then decide whether to give the group the additional time or to suggest what portion be cut.

Once in a while a band will be so good, and their music and drill excellent, that we will request that they add more time to their routine. We have to be careful, however, because quite frequently there are so many fine bands in a single parade surely we would run out of telecast time if we made many exceptions.

Macy's Thanksgiving Day Parade has built up a reputation with the band community for always giving a band its allotted television time. We pay so much attention to this portion of the show to continue this good relationship. It is also why we limit the number of bands to so few.

Bullwinkle appears to step in time to the music.

In grandstand seats, these New Yorkers enthusiastically watch the Macy's Thanksgiving Day Parade.

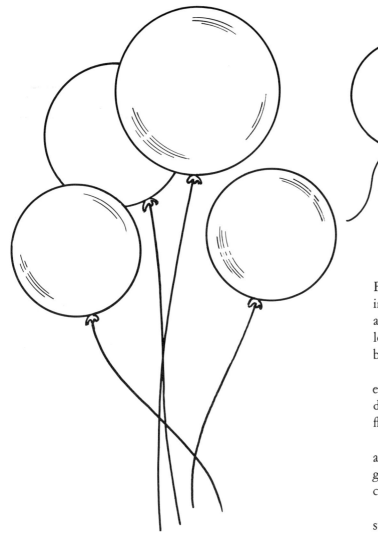

Floats in

Your Parade

Float designs are as limitless as the imagination. However, it is important that the final execution be planned practically. While a design with an ice skating rink 30 feet in diameter may be lovely, putting a surface that large on a float may prove impossible.

A local float or display company can offer the expertise necessary to produce some exciting elements for your parade. Staff designers are well versed in the limitations of an over-the-road float.

Your parade committee may choose to encourage sponsors and community groups to construct their own floats. Some basic guidelines should be offered to potential float builders that specifically relate to your parade.

Establish your theme early and require that all participants submit idea sketches to you prior to construction. A particular event may not require strict adherence, but if your parade is on July 4th, then a Christmas float would be out of place. Establish

(Opposite) Anchorage Fur Rendezvous floats depict scenes of local importance.

Parade theme can serve as a guide to corporate sponsors.

your own criteria for design, and select floats that fit that framework.

Your parade route can affect the size of the floats. If the parade must pass under a highway or overhead wires, the height of the float must be limited accordingly. The width of a float may be determined by the turning radius of a corner. Another important consideration is where you are going to build it. Remember, if you build a boat in your basement the only water it is likely to see is from a leaky pipe.

No part of the framework should be so low as to stop the float from clearing surfaces and obstacles along the parade route. Remember that the float will be lower when there are people on it.

If yours is a specialized event (i.e., water show, illuminated parade, or floral display), float entrants should be informed early. Deadlines should be established for design, construction, and delivery.

SAFETY REGULATIONS

Safety and mechanical regulations should also be established. Here are points to consider:

- Incorporate adequate brake systems as well as an emergency backup system in your design.

- Driver visibility is very important in the design of a self-contained float.

- Proper ventilation must be provided for the driver of a self-contained unit.

- The muffler must be wrapped in asbestos if it is to be near any other surface.

- Every float must have a cooling system sufficient to cool the engine.

- No decorations may block the radiator or impede the wheels or operation of the float in any way.

- Gasoline tanks on self-contained units must be large enough to hold enough gas for the unit to complete the parade.

- Batteries must be fully charged and of sufficient capacity to last the duration of the parade.

- Electrical wiring must be an approved type for your use and be well insulated.

- All wiring must be secured to the float with connections made in approved electrical boxes or devices.

- Circuits must be properly fused and grounded.

- Generators must be securely mounted away from any flammable materials and be equipped with an exhaust line.

- At least two dry chemical fire extinguishers should be on each float—one at the rear of the unit, the other with the driver.

- Any vehicles and all equipment must be checked for fuel, water, and any other vital liquids before reaching the assembly area.

- A self-contained vehicle gas tank should be positioned as far from the driver as practical and be securely bolted to the frame.

- The fuel tank must not be decorated in any way and is to be wrapped in fireproof material if it is located near the engine, exhaust, or battery.

- Flexible connections should be used on fuel tanks to avoid leaks. Gas tank caps must be vented.

- The driver of a self-contained float should have adequate space to maneuver and easy access to exits in case of emergency. Also place a carbon-monoxide detector in the driver's compartment.

- Rear lights must be required for nighttime travel.

- Safety railings, belts, back supports, or handholds must be provided for riders.

- Even if a float is self-propelled, a tow hitch must be provided. A standard hitch specification should be given to all float builders.

- Tires must be reasonably new and of good quality.

Fiberglassing is a multi-stage process.

• A spare wheel and tire should be on each float with full access available for quick change en route without the use of special equipment.

• The steering mechanism must be capable of ordinary maneuvering with no less than 45° turning radius. It is desirable to have as little play in the wheel as possible.

• Axles, bearings, and wheels must be of adequate size to support the weight of the unit and must be in good condition.

The above safety suggestions are all basic and are a composite of standard regulations published by many festivals and parades around the country. They are included here to serve as a guide in the development of your own regulations.

Floats can be built on almost anything that moves. They can be either pulled or self-propelled. Many types of floats have appeared in Macy's Thanksgiving Day Parade. Some have been pulled by cars, others by horses. Some units were built on truck beds with the driver inside. Floats can also be built on a smaller scale over a jeep-type vehicle or golf cart. We have even built floats whose only means of locomotion was a tricycle. It is also possible to build a float on a frame that is either pulled or pushed by people.

One particular small float comes to mind. This unit represented a drum and it was built over a bicycle. The driver inside had rather limited visibility. As it happened, it rained that year, so despite his short viewing range the driver was quite content. A famous band leader was to ride on top of the float in the parade. A platform had been recessed into the top of the drum

Every float begins with a preliminary sketch.

85

People-power and some imagination created this animated Ice Worm for the Anchorage Fur Rendezvous.

and a special brace was installed for his safety. Even a short stop could not buck him off.

Unfortunately, it rained on that Thanksgiving Day. Being a real trouper, however, our band leader showed up at the starting line in his band master's uniform, sharply saluted me, and then climbed the ladder to mount his float. As the unit moved into the line of march, I waved. He looked a little strange. When I reached the dispersal area later that morning, I learned that the poor man had ridden the whole line of march in water almost to his waist. We forgot to drill holes in the conductor's platform— but the driver stayed dry!

If your parade is scheduled for a specific date, it may not be possible to plan a rain date. A bad-weather plan of action should be carefully thought out.

What will you do if it rains? Snows? Will bands, floats, performers, and audience be willing to come on another day?

Are the materials used in your floats, props, and costumes able to withstand the elements if you march in the rain?

Is there adequate space to dry costumes after the show?

How safe is the route in inclement weather?

Unpleasant as it may be, all of the above should be considered.

FLOAT CONSTRUCTION

Step one in float-building is a bed, commonly called a chassis. A good, stable, 4-wheel axle and framework base is the most common variety for a street parade. Of course, many objects or vehicles can serve as a base—trailers, trucks, trolleys or boats, buses or bandwagons. Again, you can decorate anything that moves and call it a float. However, a good flatbed is easy to use and lends itself to a variety of designs.

In some cases the bed is pulled by a car, tractor, or horse. In planning a design, it is important to keep this fact in mind. The vehicle should either be part of the concept of the float or disappear visually, being a low-key model. A huge, noisy bulldozer may suit a float based on an agricultural theme. That same bulldozer would be very out of place pulling a Japanese Garden float.

Okay, now you have a flatbed. It's dull. However, take that base and let your imagination build on it. Shape, color, anima-

This design for Anheuser Busch demonstrates how a sponsor can create an appropriate float even though it does not relate to the sponsor's product.

Many crafts are utilized in float building.

This vehicle will be entirely hidden in the float.

tion, scale, and sound are the tools. A flatbed is just that—flat. Superstructures and outriggers can do a lot to change the shape of a box.

Outriggers are generally hinged platforms attached to either side of the float. They are constructed to fold down quickly and conveniently at the assembly site. They can be held in place by two chains anchored to the structure of the float. They can also be braced from underneath much like a dropleaf table with supporting beams or pipe. When in place, outriggers can totally change the shape of the bed from rectangular to round, hexagonal, or any other shape.

Outriggers can also refer to a series of minor float units connected to the main body of the float by a system of camouflaged rods and braces and riding on swivel casters.

A design incorporating auxiliary units of this type adds another dimension to the personality of a float by enabling it to extend from the middle of the street to the curb in a very dramatic way. Constructing these units sturdily enough to accommodate riders will give them the advantage of animation as well.

A superstructure adds height to a float. Towers, masts, and arches all serve to add elevation. They can be built to fold out like an origami pattern or can telescope upward—as in a series of small boxes, each rising out of a slightly larger one. The tip of such an arrangement could be a castle turret or the top of a mountain. When telescoping, remember to leave an adequate edge around each level so that the next higher one doesn't just pop right off. Each level should be secured and pinned before going on, and the whole structure should be guyed when complete.

In developing a float design you would do well to construct a small scale model first. Cardboard or heavy construction paper

Architectural superstructures.

will do. Cut the shapes as you see them on your float—rectangular base, outriggers, superstructures. Pin points of rotation. Plan how things will be folded out and how pieces will be supported. Work out animation principles. It is a great exercise, and solving a problem at this stage is much less frustrating and a whole lot cheaper than waiting until later will be.

MACY'S PARADE DESIGN STUDIO

All the floats in Macy's Thanksgiving Day Parade are designed and built by Macy's personnel in our own Parade Design Studio. Float designs vary from dragons to Hobbitts, from ice castles to cactus and sagebrush. A float built for Macy's Parade may appear once or ten times. The Turkey is an old favorite and traditionally leads the parade. Each year a different movie is represented by a float, to make the event timely and new.

To Manfred Bass, designer and builder of the Macy's Thanksgiving Day Parade floats, strict adherence to detail is of the utmost importance. Before a design is even begun an incredible amount of research is done. The design for a western float which was to carry the Lone Ranger and Tonto incorporates real sagebrush and tumbleweed. Hours were spent studying desert vegetation and land formations. Rattlesnakes were sculpted to larger-than-life size so realistically you can almost hear their hiss. Steer heads were bought at a local slaughterhouse and boiled for several days. (While I'm one of Manfred's biggest fans, I managed to stay away from the Studio during this process.)

Oversized rattlesnakes appear ready to strike on a Lone Ranger float.

Popeye's float included clamshells, brass bells, and smelly cod, all imported from Maine.

The year Popeye joined the parade, a fisherman's house was incorporated into the design of the float. Crew members sent to Maine returned with everything from small boats to seaweed, from lobster traps to clam shells and codfish—which were hung from a beam in Manfred's office till they dried properly. It's always a joy to meet with Manfred. You never know what you're going to bump into, step on, trip over, pet, or smell.

Several years ago, a float was designed to depict characters from the book *Watership Down*. This book is peopled entirely by rabbits. To the average person, "If you've seen one rabbit, . . ." but not to Mr. Bass. He went to London to meet with the producers of an animated feature based on the story. Each rabbit in *Watership Down* has a different personality, and these personalities were incorporated into the 16-foot-high rabbits on the float. The curve of an eye, the nap of the fur, the crimp in an ear, all were studied.

Of course, one cannot understand rabbits without studying them firsthand. So a petty cash voucher stating "one live rabbit, $6.98" did not surprise me in the least. By the end of the season we had a half dozen live rabbits and one beautiful float.

Sometimes, though, things can get a little too authentic. Several years ago, as Manfred tells it, Noah's Ark was being constructed for the parade. "The day we laid the keel, it began to rain.

"For a while the float's progress went unnoticed. But as the rain continued, the landlord began to get nervous. Neighbors started dropping by as construction proceeded and the rain continued for a second week.

"Soon there was 3 inches of water all over the floor of the shop, and everyone was wondering where the line was drawn between fantasy and reality."

Noah's Ark finally made it to Macy's Thanksgiving Day Parade, and no, it didn't rain that year.

Fortunately, the rain stopped, the sun came out, and the only trip the Ark had to make was to New York for the parade.

Floats in Macy's Parade are constructed of wood, steel, papier mâché, and fiberglass. Special outdoor paints are used to ensure color quality. All materials are chosen for their ability to withstand whatever the late-November weather in New York can produce.

Since all the floats are constructed in the Studio in New Jersey, each has to be engineered to collapse to an over-the-road size of 8-feet wide by 12-feet, 6-inches high. In some cases, additional outriggers and elevations are brought over on separate utility trailers, and the whole thing is assembled the morning of the parade. Some floats are as high as three or four stories and open up to 24-feet wide and 30- to 80-feet long.

All the floats are brought over in a convoy which leaves the Studio at 2 A.M. Thanksgiving morning. One tube of the Lincoln Tunnel is closed to other traffic while the convoy passes through, to be met by the New York City Police Department on the other end. The slow line of floats, props, and utilities travels up Tenth Avenue to the assembly area, led by the Police and followed by Macy's Security.

Although the streets are generally quiet at that hour of the night, a surprising number of vehicles try to cut into the convoy line. I am sure there has been more than one late-night reveler who has taken the pledge after meeting our real dragon traveling with a respectable speed toward his parade assignment.

My very first convoy is a very vivid memory: The excitement of seeing all the floats lined up in the street for the first time; how good the coffee tasted, even though it did have milk and sugar in it; the bite in the air as one final check was made before departure. It all seems to have happened yesterday. We started slowly, one unit at a time, till the whole convoy was in

Tricycle props are fun.

motion, New Jersey Police escorting us. As we approached the Thruway we passed some construction and the convoy slowed up even more. We were on the ramp heading south at a snail's pace when, suddenly, through the window on the driver's side, I saw the Tortoise speed up the ramp heading north. Before I could open my mouth, the Hare followed in hot pursuit. They had made a wrong turn and were halfway to Albany before they could turn around.

The crew works through the night to assemble the floats in time for the stepoff at 9 A.M. Every bolt must be in place. Every safety railing must be secured. Safety is of prime importance and no detail is too small to be checked, and then rechecked.

ANIMATION

Animation incorporated into a float design makes the visual appeal of the unit more interesting. Using simple rotation, a carousel can turn or a paddle wheeler can appear to propel itself along the parade route.

Toronto police precede Eaton's Parade.

A seesaw motion can focus the eye on more than one plane. This motion can be used to make a head and neck of a dragon go up and down or wag the tail of a dog. Simple animation can be accomplished manually on the float, or with a rope-and-pulley system operated by personnel located inside the float.

The Cootie float in Macy's Parade—an 18-foot-high, 22-foot-long replica of the three-inch toy—uses this simple form of animation to make the head and eyes move. The first year this unit was in the parade, however, our crew added another bit of animation on their own. All the way down the line of march they proceeded to drop plastic eggs out of the back of the Cootie's body. Fortunately, they were brightly colored eggs, and people along the line of march quickly dubbed them "Cootie eggs," and looked for them the following year.

A local hardware dealer can help translate your scale model animation into workable form, suggesting practical alternatives. Farm machinery outlets, industrial supply companies, or local mechanics can also be a good source of materials and information.

Often an everyday item like an old roller skate or skateboard wheels can be used to create the mechanism for a turntable which can then be operated manually from below or the side.

Vaughn's, Inc., a company widely known for its floats, publishes the *Manual for the Amateur Float Builder.* Simple animation is illustrated in this how-to booklet.

Animation mechanisms should be carefully thought out before being constructed. They should be built and tested prior to use in the float to avoid having to dismantle a decorative treatment because the animation needs repair. Despite the sophistication of machinery for animation, the safest way to ensure an effect isn't lost due to a malfunction is to make it people-powered.

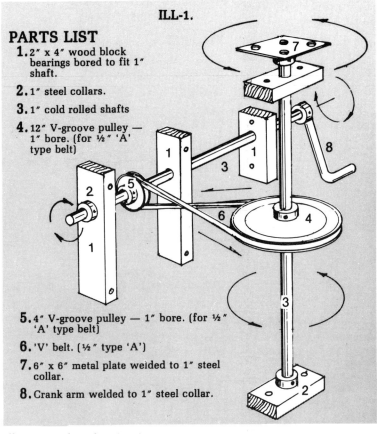

ILL-1.

PARTS LIST

1. 2" x 4" wood block bearings bored to fit 1" shaft.
2. 1" steel collars.
3. 1" cold rolled shafts
4. 12" V-groove pulley — 1" bore. (for ½" 'A' type belt)
5. 4" V-groove pulley — 1" bore. (for ½" 'A' type belt)
6. 'V' belt. (½" type 'A')
7. 6" x 6" metal plate welded to 1" steel collar.
8. Crank arm welded to 1" steel collar.

Illustration of simple animation.

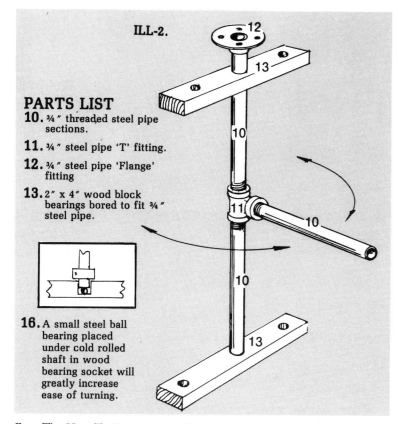

ILL-2.

PARTS LIST

10. ¾″ threaded steel pipe sections.

11. ¾″ steel pipe 'T' fitting.

12. ¾″ steel pipe 'Flange' fitting

13. 2″ x 4″ wood block bearings bored to fit ¾″ steel pipe.

16. A small steel ball bearing placed under cold rolled shaft in wood bearing socket will greatly increase ease of turning.

From The How-To-Do-It Manual for the Amateur Float Builder, *Copyright © 1978 Vaughn's Inc.*

Of course, you must make sure that the people have adequate ventilation, room to operate, and are thoroughly familiar with the animation principles.

Sculpted figures on a float add novelty to the basic design. Remember, however, that you are designing a stage set which will be seen from all sides. Sculpted forms can be created as a setting for a Queen or other celebrity, or to convey a particular visual message.

Papier mâché is a commonly used sculpting medium. To work successfully in papier mâché you should begin with an armature. A simple armature can be created by cutting out a profile of the desired figure from plywood and scaling it to the size you require for the float. Then cut out a front-view outline. Crosshatch them (fit them together at right angles) and you have a basic armature. The skeleton of a figure can also be welded steel.

Chicken wire is then shaped to the figure and nailed over the armature. When all curves are formed, the chicken wire sculpture is ready for its papier mâché skin. Remember, when finished, there should be no hexagonal chicken wire showing.

An added precaution which will protect the papier-mâché figure from possible bad weather is to coat the final product with a layer of fiberglass. This not only protects, but also can serve as a base coat of color for the finished figure when dyes are added to the resins. Resins are used in fiberglass construction when dye is added in early stages. Their use results in a pure, more lasting, color. Shellac and outdoor paint will do if weather is not a consideration.

Often when Manfred Bass designs a large sculpted figure he begins with a welded-steel armature. Papier mâché and fiberglass are then layered over the framework. When sculpting the 40-

foot long Smaug, the dragon from *The Hobbitt,* the body was hollow to allow for the pulleys and cables which animated the head and neck and also for the five people who were to do the animation. This float had the added excitement of breathing fire—well, actually it was only smoke, but was very effective nonetheless.

A sculpture can be made from a variety of other materials too. Soft sculpture created from fabric and stuffed with a wadding substance has been effectively used. An overgrown scarecrow with stuffed head and body can be created well. Again, you can get as complicated or stay as simple as your budget, time, and imagination will allow.

Some float-building companies have decorative shapes available molded in papier mâché for float use. There are kits available also for the do-it-yourselfer that include superstructure, decorated background, props, floral sheeting, fringe, festooning, artificial flowers, lettering, and signs. Instructions for preparation of trailer bed and framework are also included.

Color and shine make a float exciting as well. Foil or mirrored surfaces, sparkle sheeting, and glitter attract the eye, and strong colors make a unit visually appealing. All exposed surfaces must be either painted or covered. You can use polypetal sheeting, artificial or real flowers, paint, fabrics, fringe, or colored paper. Just remember that the float will be viewed from all sides. A fabric skirt or one of fringe will hide the wheels and give the illusion of floating. Plan colors carefully. Good, strong colors can make a float stand out against the drab color of the pavement. Earthy colors tend to blend in with the pavement and the float will not stand out as well.

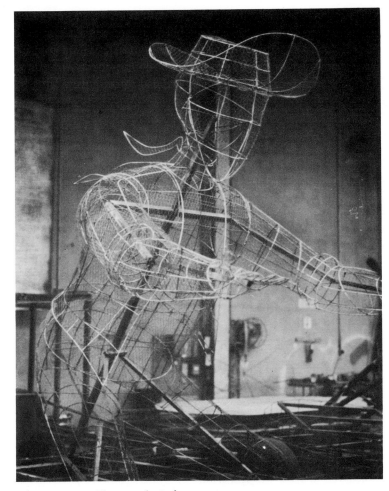

Float armature illustrates basic form.

SPECIAL FLOATS

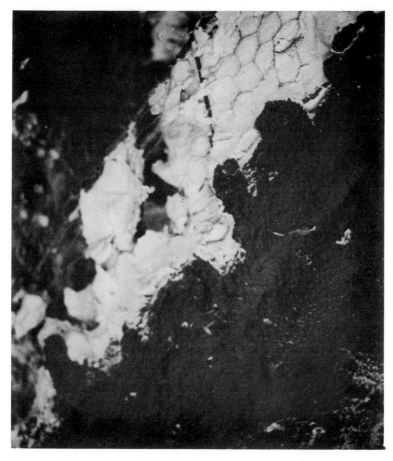

Cocooning is layered over chicken-wire frame.

Upon request, the Pasadena Tournament of Roses Association will send you information specifically relating to the construction of Rose Parade floats. The Tournament of Roses judges disqualify any float not completely covered with organic material. All their units are self-propelled, being built on a stripped-down vehicle chassis.

Basic framing and preparation is much the same as for a non-floral float. However, when the chicken-wire stage is completed, a process called "cocooning" takes place. This involves spraying a polyvinyl material over the wire mesh to provide a surface on which to glue flowers. Papier mâché is used for more detailed shapes.

The whole unit is painted in the same colors as the planned floral covering. Flowers are then attached to the cocooned surface of the float with a plastic rubber-base glue. Several types of glue are used, depending upon the organic material involved. Some very delicate flowers are actually placed in vials of chemically treated water and are sunk into the surface of the float. Because of the perishable materials used, floats are not completed more than a few hours before the parade. A great deal of labor is necessary to ready them. Millions of blossoms are used.

A nighttime parade offers other problems. A wonderfully decorated float may look great in daylight but strong artificial light may change its whole appearance. Theatrical lighting is a whole field in itself. The interaction between artificial light and color is complex. If you are creating a float for a nighttime parade, you would do well to enlist the help of an electrician with some theatrical background. You may also want to test paint colors in artificial light before they are applied to your design.

Vehicle is buried within the float.

Here are some helpful hints:

1. Place lights so that rays flow back along the contours and dimensions of the float. The less light on the pavement or other units, the more efficiently the unit is illuminated.

2. No lights should shine at spectators.

3. Set colors into float decoration and highlight them with white light.

4. Strings of lights can be used to outline the float and provide illumination. Clear glass bulbs with the filaments exposed are recommended. They have a twinkling effect.

5. Neon lights can provide colorful and varied accents.

6. Figures on the float should be spotlighted.

All the lighting should be carefully planned ahead of time. It should be incorporated into the concept for the float and

This Orange Bowl Illuminated Parade float shows many small units in tandem telling a story.

should not be included as an afterthought. Proper power sources should be researched and tested. Light tests should be made often with all parts of the veneer prior to final application.

Nighttime water parades are exceptionally lovely, as the reflected lights double the impact of the floats. Much simpler frames can be constructed for a strictly illuminated water show. Lights strung to conform to specific shapes can be dramatic and can also be animated.

If you are planning a nighttime event, or any type of parade for that matter, and you need direction, don't be timid about reaching out to someone who runs an event you admire and ask for information. The worst thing that could happen is that the person will say no. More often than not, you will probably come away with more than you need. Sharing of information and ideas helps us all to grow. One thing, though: Don't call a parade director two weeks before his event and expect the kind of attention you would get six months later.

In planning float designs you should decide whether the unit will carry a queen or a performing group. Appropriate staging areas should be included.

Don't forget the logo. Signs on floats should be limited to certain areas. A signature on the front of the float or on each side along the bed is visible and will not interfere with the design.

Macy's has very strict guidelines about commercial entries in the Thanksgiving Day Parade. Float designs are institutional in nature, and no product can be represented literally. In other words, we work with potential sponsors to develop a float design which will be appropriate for the parade and the sponsor as well.

For example, one year the Bulova Watch Company was considering participation in Macy's Parade. We couldn't have a huge wrist watch on a float, so we did a little research to find

The hands of time are added to Macy's Bulova float.

children's stories which related to time. Our Cinderella float was the result. A pumpkin coach pulled by wonderful sculpted horses appears ready to take Cinderella away from the ball as the clock prepares to strike midnight. Appropriate. Subtle.

Parade audiences are out there to be entertained, not sold. A commercial sponsor can gain more by being an integral part of the show than by being blatantly commercial. In televised shows like Macy's Parade or the Orange Bowl, viewers may use commercial time to step away from the television. Establish commercial guidelines for your parade, and make sure float builders as well as potential sponsors are aware of them. It is your event and you should control its development.

Often a neighboring community will have a float unit built for its own festival or parade celebration. An invitation for this unit to appear in your parade may result in a reciprocal arrangement. This can serve to enhance the stature and exposure of your event.

One word of caution, however. I know that many parades allow trinkets or promotional items to be tossed to spectators from float units. Consider this very carefully and consult your local police. My greatest fear is that in their enthusiasm to catch a bauble, the crowds may surge and someone may be injured. In New York, where we estimate that two to three million spectators line the parade route, we are forbidden from distributing anything along the line of march for just this reason.

Completed clock tower is only a small part of the Cinderella Float in Macy's Thanksgiving Day Parade.

People

in Your Parade

The most colorful, interesting, indestructible animation on floats or on the street comes from the people in your parade. A careful blending of props, stages, and people will make your parade a hit. It is the balance that is important. A parade made up only of marchers is dull, a parade only of floats is dull. A parade only of balloons is monotonous. While music is the thread holding a parade together, and floats and balloons the pearls, people are the shine.

When a float is designed to hold riders, careful consideration must be given to the appropriate costuming of those float riders. Costumes should be complementary not only in design but in color as well.

Costumes should be as carefully selected as any other portion of float decor. Of course, budget comes into play here, as well. But if you are creating the ground rules, costume coordination should be one of them. Expensive costumes not properly coordinated to the entire unit can be just as distracting.

(Opposite) Appropriately costumed royalty watch the Minneapolis Aquatennial Parade from a choice location.

Sadly, not enough attention is given to costuming in a parade. Frequently, float riders will adorn a float in what would be lovely gowns in a social situation. Placed on a float and elevated over the spectators, all flaws are very obvious. For example, something as simple as a short petticoat under a long dress has made me cringe when viewing a parade.

There is no need to buy or rent costumes from a professional costumer—although there is also no reason not to. Community groups or school sewing classes may costume a float using local talent very successfully. Some considerations here include theme, weather conditions (warm, cold, how will they withstand rain, snow), color, and durability. Will costumes be used again? Will they be worn by someone else?

In general, everyone who rides or accompanies a float should know his or her position and its limitations. Choreographers recruited from local dancing schools can be of assistance here. It is advisable to spend some time with your Queen to rehearse, discussing where and how to stand, how to smile, the proper wave so her arm won't fall off, and how to hang on gracefully when the float stops short.

Macy's Thanksgiving Day Parade also includes float escorts. The theory here is to extend the excitement of the float right to the curb. Escorts are appropriately costumed to complement each float. With proper choreography and a performance, the people in your parade will be a very entertaining part of the show.

Traditional costumes are in order at the Frankenmuth Bavarian Festival.

The Klompen Dancers, in authentic costume, create animation and variety in the Holland, Michigan, Tulip Time Festival Parade.

10

V.I.P.'s
and Other Guests

Everyone in your parade is important. The person driving the floats, the people in the equestrian act, and the performing talent all play a part in the success of your show.

Pretty girls are an asset to any show. The selection of the Queen can be another opportunity to involve the community in your event. The selection process and coronation ceremonies are usually held prior to a parade and can also be a source of revenue. To ride in the parade may be the Queen's first official duty. Sometimes a King is also chosen from the business community or from the organization producing the event. Both the King and Queen, as well as their Court, are usually placed together on a float specially designed for them.

Since the person selected as Queen in the promotion of your parade will be spokesperson for your community, great care must be used in selecting her. The selection process should be a fair evaluation of each candidates poise, speaking voice, and photogenic qualities. Ground rules should be established regard-

(*Opposite*) *Night parades present special lighting problems.*

ing the eligibility of contestants: residency requirements, age, academic levels, sponsorship limitations. Judging should be done impartially after these ground rules have been established so that no question of eligibility can affect the reign of your Queen and her Court.

Your community, no matter what size, will have its share of local celebrities. These may include the mayor, director of the chamber of commerce, a prominent citizen who happens to collect antique cars, or someone from the community who has won national fame with a major baseball team or in the theatre.

Local celebrities can be found everywhere.

Specialty groups like these Shrine Keystone Kops are a fun parade element.

A couple of Octobers ago, I was visiting a marching band in Glasgow, Kentucky. It was quite close to Thanksgiving and, as usual, I was in contact with my office several times a day. I had stopped at a pay phone to make one such call when I learned that Bucky Dent, of New York Yankees fame, had agreed to ride in the Macy's Parade. I went back to the car quite pleased and announced the news to the band director and his wife. They looked at me incredulously, then pointed out that Bucky came from Horse Creek, Kentucky. I laughed at the coinci-dence—I had called from his home state and gotten the news. I stopped laughing when I noticed the name over the general store across the road, the "Horse Creek General Store." Amazing, but true, as the saying goes.

Traveling around the country to visit parade bands has taken me to a wide variety of communities. At first I was surprised when local residents would point out that a famous movie personality, television performer, or sports figure had been born there. In many cases parents and cousins still lived there. I now

Mr. Fur Face, winner of the best overall beard of Miners and Trappers Ball, riding in the Anchorage Fur Rendez-vous.

Eaton's Santa Claus Parade is telecast in Canada and the United States.

realize this is more the rule than the exception. Your town may also have a resident hero who can be persuaded to come home to appear in a parade which may very well pass right in front of the old homestead.

The International Festivals Association lists many festivals and parade events around the country. An invitation to the reigning representatives of a number of them can add much to your parade. Each queen and escort should ride a float in your parade and receive all the social benefits of such a visit as well. Your royalty would, in turn, visit each to reciprocate. This schedule could be part of a year-long itinerary. An exchange program of this nature affords your publicity committee the opportunity to attract press interest at home with the arrival of out-of-town guests. Press coverage should also be encouraged in other areas, too.

If there is a Civic Center or University in your town, you should check with them to see if a concert or other special performance is planned. In this way, performers who may be in the area can be invited to appear in your parade to promote their show.

Local television and radio stations quite often will provide performers to appear in a parade and then will proceed to cover the event. The guest personalities may also use their broadcast visibility to promote their appearance in your event as well.

Television coverage will add to the promotional appeal of a parade, both to performers and sponsors. It may also add some operational headaches too, but the exposure is well worth the effort. Again, the more prestigious your event becomes, the easier it will be to attract participants. Learning how to say no gracefully will then be part of your planning.

11

Everyone

Loves the Clowns

Clowns add a very special dimension to a parade. The warmth, the humor, the one-to-one contact with the audience makes the parade a participatory experience. Watching a parade that is a continuous panorama is certainly enjoyable, but have a clown shake your hand or throw confetti at you and you are part of the show.

Clowns may not always fit the format of a parade. The Tournament of Roses Parade, for example, is rather formal in its content. However, clowns do add spontaneity and audience contact and should be included if your format permits.

Most of Macy's clowns are either employees or family or friends of employees. Many have never clowned before. Many clown only on Thanksgiving Day. Some are clowns all year long. Macy's boasts of having the world's largest assembly of clowns in the Thanksgiving Day Parade. There are about 700, ranging in age from eight to eighty.

Several years ago one of our employees asked if a friend

(Opposite) Clever clown costumes.

Clowns and clown vehicles can be fun in a parade. If time permits, skits can be performed but should not impede the progress of the parade.

Clowns should be ready to regroup and move on as instructed. The High Bawll Hobos effectively combine skits and props.

could join him in the parade as a clown. After accepting the friend's application, we discovered that she was seventy years old. Now, two and one-half miles is a nice, healthy walk if you're in good shape, but the thought of a seventy-year-old clown made me a little nervous.

Not only was I wrong about her being able to finish the route that year, but she has been coming back to join us again and again. This charming lady begins training for her parade appearance about the beginning of September. She starts out by walking one-half mile, then gradually increases the distance each day until she has reached two and one-half miles. She tells me that she doesn't plan to think about retiring from the parade until she's "100 years young." The love and joy she absorbs each year from the children watching the parade will surely sustain her till then.

Your community may have its own share of clowns. Clown clubs have been formed in many areas of the country and the Clowns of America organization based in Chicago is always adding new chapters. These groups generally include people whose interest in clowning brings them together. They exchange ideas, skills, and stories. Often they will establish a program of hospital, nursing home, and day-care center visits as a service to the community.

Not everyone can be a clown. Some of the clowns in Macy's Parade are ordinary people in makeup and costume who enjoy the anonymity of the role. They have a good time and go home with the knowledge that they have made the day special for some.

You can be taught some of the basic information needed to develop a clown personality. But clowning itself cannot be taught; it must be a part of you. We all have a little clown in us, but only the rare personality becomes an established clown.

Mr. Chuck, Macy's official clown.

Mr. Chuck, Macy's official clown, offers some advice for the novice: First, think about the type of clown best suited to you physically and in personality. Some research here will help. Explore the many types—rustic, pathetic, august. Consider the hobo, the Pierrot, the fat clown, the clown on stilts, and the musical clown. There are many others worth discovering.

Once you have selected your character, forget you are Stanley Livingston and keep in mind that you are now "Stan the Man," *clown extraordinaire.* The clown is the medium, and the audience is not interested in who the clown is, but what he does and how he does it.

CLOWN MAKEUP

A clown sometimes changes his costume, often his act, but the one thing a clown never changes is his makeup. As Mr. Chuck points out, a clown's makeup is very personal. The contours of his face automatically make it so. The same makeup will look different on two faces.

Experiment with makeup on yourself or a friend. Collect pictures and posters of clowns for easy reference. You are not copying, you are learning. Imitating an established clown is as unnecessary as it is wrong. *Your* personality and face are special, too.

Here are some basic things you should know about the application of clown makeup. They key word here is *exaggerate.*

1. Put on any parts of your costume that go over your head before you apply makeup. Place a towel or drape a large cloth over your shoulders to protect your costume from loose powder or spills. Cover or pin back your hair to keep it out of the way.

2. Always start at the top of your face and work downward.

3. Lightly apply cold cream to the face, wiping off the excess, to prevent makeup from collecting in the pores.

4. If you are going to be a "white-faced" clown, begin by dotting the face with small quantities of clown white base. Apply in circular motions to cover the face evenly. Remember the ears and back of the neck. Pat with hands for an even, matte finish.

5. Now comes the fun part. Powder the whole face liberally, brushing off the excess, to set the makeup.

This brings visions of people being smacked with huge powder puffs and disappearing in a cloud, as someone yells "makeup!" Actually, it's not really as exciting as all that. I've watched Mr. Chuck apply his makeup, and he uses a baby sock filled with talcum powder and pats all over gently.

6. Using grease pencils, start above the eye. Raise the eyebrows and extend the eyes, creating any shape you wish. Don't neglect the forehead area. Fill in with color. Powder the new areas.

7. Now, under the eyes, fill in the eye socket with color. Powder. Line the eye with colored pencil. Add teardrops,

laugh lines, flowers, etc. Powder. You may have noticed that after every step Mr. Chuck powders. This helps set the colors. Only the new areas are powdered, and excess is brushed off.

8. Next is the nose. If you plan to use a fake nose, wait until your makeup is complete before putting it on.

If you plan to paint the nose, start at the bridge and outline the shape you desire, then fill with color. Be very careful to complete the underneath portion of the nose. Remember, most of your audience is down below looking up. Powder.

9. Now you are ready for the mouth, and some decision making. Will you be a happy clown or a sad clown? Will the mouth go up or down? Once you have created the shape with pencil or brush, apply color from the lips outward and fill in the area. Powder and brush.

In developing your face, you can either make up or ignore cheeks or chin. Also, it is not necessary to start with a completely white face. You may choose to use white as an accent over the eyes or at the mouth. Practice and experimentation will determine the right face for you.

10. When you are ready to take the makeup off, use plenty of cold cream or baby oil.

Your costume may be bought, rented, or already in your closet. It should reflect the character you have become. Again, anything exaggerated—oversized pants, wide ties, loud stripes—lends itself to a costume. Remember, though, you'll be wearing the costume for the whole parade. It must be able to withstand a lot of handshaking and enthusiastic children who will pull at it, and it must be light enough not to be physically exhausting for you.

Once you have established your character, you may then wish to include juggling, mime, or magic. Skits can be developed to include two or more clowns and the audience as well. A good prop house catalog can give you an idea of the wealth of props available, from plastic foam barbells to invisible dogs. Learning pratfalls and learning to ride a unicycle all add to the show.

An amateur clown is advised to pick a simple routine for a parade and stick to it. Do it over and over. After all, you have a new audience every hundred feet or so. They will not have seen you before and you'll be refining your act as you go.

Pay no attention to other clowns and do not laugh at them unless you are working a skit together. Your attention should be entirely on the audience. In this way you build up the illusion that you, the clown, are normal, and that it's the audience that has the problem.

Please remember, however, that some children are afraid of clowns. Do not try to convince them you are a friend if they are frightened. Just move on, the rest of your audience is waiting.

Clowns prepare.

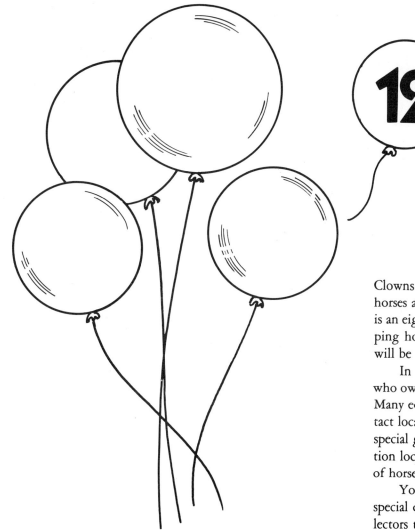

Other Units

Clowns are very special in a parade. So are horses. Beautiful horses and beautiful riders add elegance to a parade. Whether it is an eight-horse Clydesdale hitch or a group of stately high-stepping horses ridden by elegantly costumed young women, you will be rewarded by spectator enthusiasm.

In most areas of the country there are hobby equestrians who own fine horses, beautiful trappings, and colorful costumes. Many equestrians are most willing to show off in a parade. Contact local riding stables or private owners for information about special groups in your area. The American Horse Show Association located in New York can also provide you with the names of horses and owners in your area.

You may require a special vehicle for the mayor or other special dignitary. You'll be surprised how many vintage-car collectors there are across the country.

Not only vintage cars, but specialty cars like the Excalibur make wonderful additions to a parade. New car dealers may also

(Opposite) *Fleet of small cars appeared in the Cherry Festival Parade courtesy of the Squirt Soft Drink Company.*

be willing to allow their product to be seen in a parade as a promotional opportunity.

Your particular state's chapter of the Automobile Club of America can be an excellent guide to specialty units. Often, they will cooperate with you to provide emergency standby service as well. It is worth a call to explore what types of involvement are available.

Horse drawn cart at the Frankenmuth Bavarian Festival.

Floats like this little choo-choo are great crowd pleasers.

Balloons

The balloons in Macy's Parade are bigger and better than any in the world. I say this without hesitation because I love them the best. Each balloon has its own captain also. Balloon captains, however, require a certain amount of skill. Most have been in the parade and have had experience as a balloon handler. Goodyear Aerospace builds these giants exclusively for Macy's and sends a team of engineers to New York each year. They arrive several days before the parade and meet with the captains.

These giant balloons are manipulated from the ground like puppets. They wave, bow, dip, and bob on cue. The captain must understand how to make all of this happen. The following are part of the balloon captain's instructions to let you see how it's done.

One fall, I went to Rockmark, Georgia, to witness the test flight of the new Superman balloon. On the day of the test, tension was like static electricity in the air. The Goodyear engineers had begun inflating him at 8:30 A.M. with a mixture of helium

(Opposite) Superman balloon soars high during test flight.

and air. As each compartment was inflated, the scope of the figure became apparent. First, Superman's head and shoulders reared up from the tarpaulin. Then he grew bigger and stronger and more powerful. I believed in Superman, along with the hundreds of schoolchildren on hand, along with the football team members who were trying to keep him from leaping in a single bound, along with the marching band, which struck up and played as the nets were pulled from his massive body and he rose soaring into the crisp Georgian autumn sunshine. We all believed.

BAD WEATHER

As I watched the children carry on and scream each time the Superman balloon dipped in their direction, I remembered the very wet, cold parade day two years before. Not only was it cold and rainy, but the gusts of wind were unpredictable and strong. On that particular Thanksgiving Day, our Snoopy balloon was hit by a gust of wind and was punctured. Our crew, always quick to react, pulled the release patches to free the remaining helium so the balloon could be safely moved aside, as the rest of the parade went by. As the first, second, and third patches were pulled and Snoopy began to deflate, a little girl riding on her father's shoulder and clutching her Snoopy doll, began screaming hysterically, "Why are they killing Snoopy? Why are they doing that to him?" When I turned from her, I found I was crying, too.

No year has been as emotional for me as the year the balloons didn't fly. In 1971, all the weather forecasts for parade day were bad. Cold, rain, and sleet were promised. Bad weather plans were set into motion. Mummers' feathers would be shielded from the elements downtown. Performers, being the troupers

Snoopy is a longtime favorite in Macy's Parade.

that they are, chose to report to the parade assembly area because "the show must go on...." Floats arrived early from Hoboken to begin being set up. Only at this point—about 3:00 A.M.—were we told that, due to the over-100-mile-per-hour winds gusting all night and the limited amount of sandbags, the Goodyear crew had been unable to inflate the balloons. We watched as an attempt was made to inflate a portion of Underdog. Within minutes 50-pound sandbags were being hurled about the street like bits of paper.

Bernie Sklar had once confided a nightmare to me: "Being all prepared, dressed in my uniform, and arriving at the assembly area only to find the street empty." My feelings upon arrival at the assembly area on that Thanksgiving Day in 1971 were as close to that nightmare as I could imagine. On 77th Street, between Central Park West and Columbus Avenue lay the flattened balloons battered into the pavement by the driving rain. Manfred Bass and his crew, working furiously to assemble the floats, had only half finished. The parade was to start in an hour. I watched as they raised the huge Rainbow Float which was to frame Tommy Tune and the dancers from the film "The Boyfriend." The rainbow became a sail, caught in the high winds, and very nearly went down the route alone....

Enough of that. The good has far outweighed the bad. Watching one of Macy's giant balloons soar as it is warmed by a thin November sun makes you feel like a child again, if only for a moment. Who says fantasies shouldn't be bigger than life?

However fanciful, balloons are serious business with our parade. Each spring, trees along the route are pruned by the Department of Parks, to ensure that no sharp branches protrude.

Underdog poses on 77th Street.

PROPER WAY

Ropes should not extend too far
in front or too far behind balloon.

All ropes should be fairly taut with
just a slight pull on them. If your
rope becomes loose, move out slightly.
Call for a Goodyear man or a Macy's
group leader if you need help.

OBSERVE THE FOLLOWING:

1. Do not walk over or cross your line with anyone else's.

2. Handlers walking along curbs must watch for trees, light poles,
    and other obstructions.

3. The balloons absolutely cannot stop at any intersections. You
    must hurry them along.

4. Watch for hand signals from the Goodyear and Macy's men as the
    noise is quite loud.

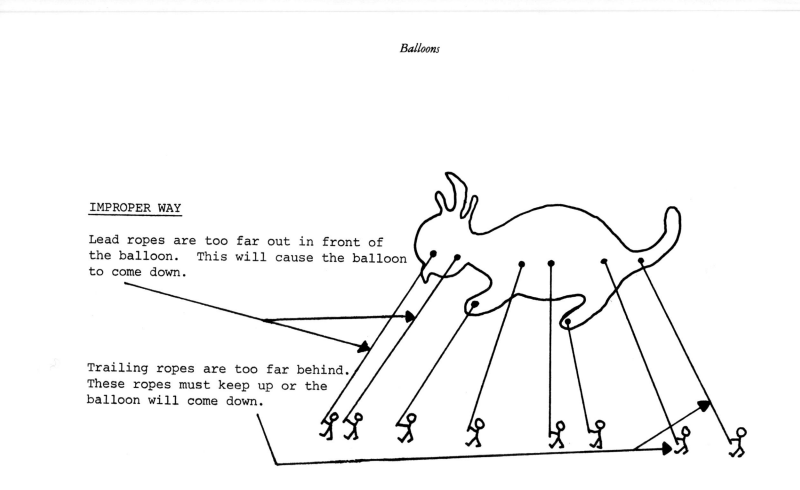

IMPROPER WAY

Lead ropes are too far out in front of
the balloon. This will cause the balloon
to come down.

Trailing ropes are too far behind.
These ropes must keep up or the
balloon will come down.

This information is distributed to all balloon handlers in the Macy's Parade.

Early in October, Macy's representatives as well as Goodyear engineers, survey the entire parade route. Each lamppost, traffic signal and overhead cable is inspected. We contract to have over 60 poles and signals either turned out of the way or removed entirely to ensure the safety of our flying giants. Over 100,000 cubic feet of helium is ordered.

Goodyear engineers arrive early to meet with our balloon captains and go over every possible detail. Handlers are recruited from Macy's personnel with careful attention to ensure that no one under 120 pounds is signed up. The balloons are designed to have no more than 150–300 pound lift. This means that if the lift is 150 pounds, theoretically a 150-pound person could hold it down. None of us is prepared to test this fact, however. It is difficult to imagine Underdog being walked down the route by one person—no matter what size that person.

In the years since 1927 when the first of our balloons delighted New Yorkers, 92 balloons have been built by Goodyear for the Macy's Parade. This long-standing exclusive relationship has continued successfully even though the responsibility for actual construction is now part of the Goodyear Aerospace Division. It's a long way from automobile tires, heavy lifting bags, expulsion bladders and giant liquid storage tanks to Kermit the Frog.

There are other companies that construct giant inflatables of varying sizes. Some balloons fly when filled with helium and some are made to ride on beds like floats. A call to the International Festivals Association should provide the names of such companies. Many also rent inflated figures and have a ready stock on hand. Others will only build to your specifications. It is also possible to rent an entire parade of these units as well.

Giant balloons have appeared in Macy's Parade since 1927.

Hot-air balloons add another dimension to a festival.

14

How Much
Will It Cost?

A favorite question when I've been interviewed about the parade is "How much does it cost?" Budget planning will play an important part in your event too. Not only *how much,* but *how* is important as well. Local events can be funded in several ways. Assuming that you do not have an angel ready, pen poised, to write out a check to cover the show, some salesmanship will be required.

Often a city will not only endorse an event that it feels will be beneficial to the community, but will also give financial support. The promotional value of swelling the population for a parade is tremendous, not only in prestige, but in business generated. It is to the city's advantage, then, to be as supportive as possible to make the event a success.

Revenue raising methods can include:

1. Reviewing-stand ticket sales—recognizing the importance of local support, spectators purchase grandstand tickets.

(Opposite) Corporate-sponsored floats help offset parade expenses.

2. Programs or journals—sell such booklets, which include advertising by community businesses and show the parade lineup, plus information about participating units. This can be very successful.

3. Other product sales—buttons, pennants, T-shirts, sun visors, totebags, coffee mugs, pens, ashtrays, etc., or anything imprinted with the logo of your event can be a phenomenal source of dollars. If it is personalized with a name or photo, all the better.

4. Arrange for the parade floats to be displayed either before or after the parade in an area set aside for this purpose. Charge admission and let visitors take pictures of their children and friends on the floats.

5. Business sponsorship of parade units or corporate contributions. Here it will be necessary to show the value the sponsor will be getting for his investment. This may be difficult for a first-time event, but as its success grows your parade will attract sponsors on its merits as a promotional vehicle.

6. If a particular corporate sponsor wishes to underwrite the entire event, then a big headache is out of the way. Such is the case with Eaton's Parade in Toronto, and, of course, Macy's Parade in New York.

7. A parade may also be run by a city for its own promotional purposes and may not encourage commercial sponsors at all.

Folks love to take pictures.

The finance committee should include members who are active in the business community or who have been involved in successful charitable campaigns. The budget should include all anticipated revenues and expenses and should provide for contingencies. Proper books should be set up and maintained faithfully. An accountant's services are advisable.

Expenses may include:

- Professional fees for artists, performers, etc.

- Expense payments to non-professional artists, performers, etc.

- Equipment and space rental fees

- Decor expenses

- Advertising and promotion (10 to 15 percent of total projected revenues)

- Hospitality and entertainment for special guests

- Salaries for non-volunteer workers and technicians

- Contingencies

Again, the methods for financing your event are only limited by the committee's experience and imagination. A simple and most original idea for fund-raising I learned from a high school band from Minnesota. The group had to raise a great deal of money to come to New York for the Thanksgiving Day Parade and to complete an education tour of Washington, D.C. When we visited the school to see their rehearsal, we asked how the band had been able to fund the trip.

"Why we sold Band-Aids, of course," I was told. Each student in the band had gone out into the community and sold Band-Aids door-to-door for one dollar apiece. Over ten thousand dollars was raised in the first two days of the campaign.

The creation of a parade organization which encourages membership throughout the year is another good method for raising funds. A token membership fee gives the production team a vested interest in the success of the event as well.

If the parade organization creates an appropriate logo, that identification can become a source of revenue. As licenses for its use are sold, proceeds from the fees can offset parade costs. Promotional benefits are also accrued by the exposure of event memorabilia.

A ready market for such items are the members of the school bands you bring to your community. A collection of T-shirts or buttons from places they have performed is a wonderful way to show off to friends. Items that can be personalized inexpensively and quickly tend to make good sales.

How and when these items are available for purchase is also important. The parade headquarters, a very accessible place to all participants, should be a location where purchases can be made. Prior to parade day, grandstand tickets may be sold here. Everyone who comes in to buy a ticket is a potential customer for the souvenir catalog, a pennant, or a T-shirt.

15

Promotion and Publicity

If a single word were chosen to describe the Macy's Parade, it would have to be *quality*. There is a simple ground rule about appearance in the parade: If you are not good, you are not in it.

It is this type of reputation that has enabled the Macy's Parade to perpetuate a tradition that is unique. We constantly strive to maintain quality. The musicians are the best; the talent is outstanding; the floats are first class; and the weather, . . . well, you can't always have everything.

Everyone loves a parade, and Macy's has become the one that America watches to kick off the holiday season. Although television coverage is extensive on the day of the parade, it's newspapers and magazines that keep the parade in the public eye on a year-round basis.

Macy's subscribes to a clipping service. Every mention of Macy's Thanksgiving Day Parade in papers anywhere in North America is clipped and sent to the store. In one year, over 3,000 clippings were received. These included every state, Canada,

(Opposite) A good slogan can do wonders for publicity.

139

Puerto Rico, and Mexico. The total circulation of all these presses was over 278-million readers. With an estimated 80-million television viewers and three million or so people who actually see the parade live on Thanksgiving Day, that's a pretty impressive number—and it all started as a local parade.

Getting the word out and generating enthusiasm is of prime importance to the success of any event. Whether a volunteer committee does the job or an agency is hired, promotion and publicity should be planned as early as possible.

The timing of promotion and publicity is very important. The committee should prepare a calendar of activities executed in logical sequence. Enough lead time should be allowed for preparation and organization of each press event.

The International Festivals Association offers some techniques used successfully by promotion and publicity committees around the country. Consider the following: Inform local church groups, service clubs, school organizations, and the business community about plans for the event.

The members of your committee should establish a liaison with the local media. Keep them informed of the progress of the event. Arrange for special stories about the event to be broadcast or printed at suitable intervals. Perhaps even invite someone from the press to be part of the committee.

Distribute news releases, with photos, if possible, not only to local media but also to media in surrounding areas. There is no reason why you should not use a wire service as well. Quite often Associated Press or United Press International will pick up a story on a local event from the local media. It may then be printed in papers all over the country. There is the chance they will take it from the release you provide them as well. The wider the interest in your event, the more successful it becomes.

Releases should be planned so that separate announcements are made about different aspects of the event. Depending upon the size of your community and the rapport of your publicity committee with the press, you may elect to hold press conferences to announce major news about your parade.

Programs are a good source of publicity, as well as generating revenues. They should give information about the entire event, a timetable, and the location of the parade route, as well as highlighting participants. They can also give credit to those who have contributed time, money, or services.

Posters, brochures, pamphlets, or flyers should be designed and distributed in your community and surrounding areas.

INVOLVING THE BUSINESS COMMUNITY

Arrange for local businesses to help promote the event. See if you can get your logo on locally produced products, books of matches, or placemats. It is worth exploring the cost of a special postage slug which would carry news of your event on every piece of metered mail.

Any business or organization participating should be required to participate in the promotion, by displaying posters or giving out brochures at point of sale, or including mention of their participation in any print or broadcast advertising they may schedule prior to the event.

When a local television station does a feature story on the festival, distribute copies to surrounding communities. Distribute press information on all cultural and ethnic organizations participating in your parade. Generate press interest in the particular aspects of the event which encourage community involvement—construction of floats, rehearsal of marchers or performers, selection of a queen, etc.

Create and place advertising in newspapers, radio, and television. Remember that the Automobile Club of America sends out a newspaper to 21-million subscribers all over the country. Consider informing their Public Relations office about your event.

Concentrate your heaviest advertising two weeks prior to the event, and arrange for photo documentation of your event. Not only will it provide news items during the show, but will prove useful for future parades as well.

Your press release should call immediate attention to what is happening in your event, as is illustrated in the heading below.

INTERNATIONAL FREEDOM FESTIVAL NEWS RELEASE

1981 WHEELS OF FREEDOM AUTOMOBILE SHOW AND PARADE

Where else but in the "Motor City" could you find 150 antique automobiles in a spectacular day-long show and parade? How about in Detroit and Windsor?

Antique car buffs, parade lovers and families looking for weekend fun will all enjoy the second annual "Wheels of Freedom Automobile Show & Parade" on Saturday, June 27 as part of the 1981 International Freedom Festival.

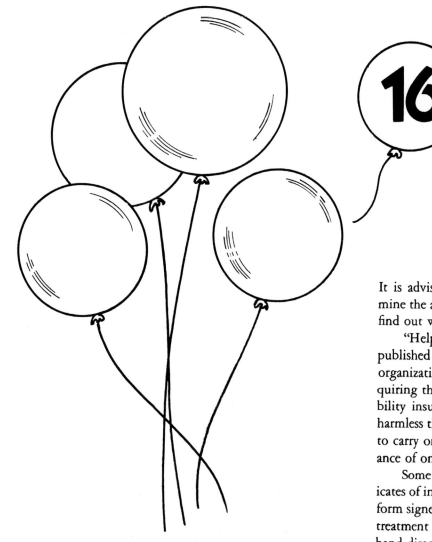

16

Insurance

It is advisable to consult an insurance representative to determine the amount of risk connected with your type of parade and find out what liability insurance would cost.

"Helpful Hints and Hows in Festival/ Parade Planning," published by the Valley Decorating Company, recommends that organizations which sponsor parades protect themselves by requiring the sponsor of each float or other entry to purchase liability insurance, not only to protect the sponsor but to hold harmless the host organization. Community organizations set up to carry on a festival on an annual basis all have liability insurance of one type or another.

Some events also require that marching bands submit certificates of insurance as well. It may be advisable to require a release form signed by each band member's parents to authorize medical treatment in case of an emergency. These can be retained by the band director.

It doesn't cost anything to explore what coverage is advis-

(Opposite) Utilize all your resources.

able. There is no point ignoring this issue, especially when you can rather easily determine the risks and protect yourself, your participants and your community.

Insurance gives you an added measure of security, by providing protection for little fellows like this one.

BAND SELECTION CRITERIA

When considering bands for selection for a Festival Parade, the following criteria are considered. It is not necessary that a band meet all the criteria. However, a band meeting the greatest number of these criteria would be considered to be the most obvious choice.

1. Minimum size of block: 80 playing members.
2. Audience interest potential of auxiliary groups is a consideration.
3. A balanced marching instrumentation appropriate to the music being performed is a determining factor.
4. All members of the organization should be appropriately and attractively uniformed and/or costumed.
5. The band should have received a first-division rating (superior) at a recent major marching contest.
6. Recent previous participation in another parade of national significance is helpful.
7. The band should have the ability to provide evidence of high standards of musical and marching performance.

8. Uniqueness of presentation is highly desirable.
9. The excellence of the supporting documents and photographs submitted with the application is a factor in the band's selection.

NOTE

1. All applicants must include a letter of approval from the high school principal or superintendent.
2. All applicants must include evidence of public liability insurance.

In addition to overall event insurance coverage, you can request that participants provide evidence of public liability, as shown in the above band information sheet.

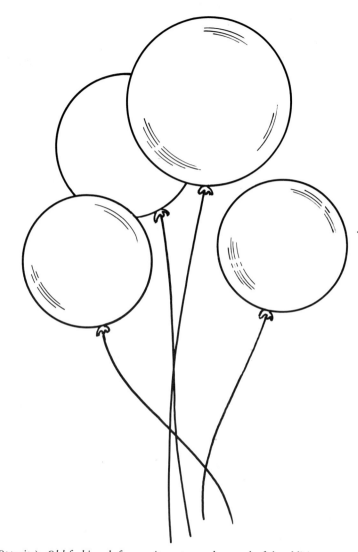

17

What about Next Year?

With a little luck, your event will be a big success. The decision whether or not to continue it as an annual event may very well be based on the degree of its success.

A postmortem meeting of all committees should be held while the parade is fresh in everyone's mind. Every aspect of parade planning and operation should be reviewed. This is a good time for some backslapping. However, a postmortem session is primarily a dissection of the whole event—good *and* bad.

All problems should be brought up and solutions suggested. All areas should be critiqued honestly. If the event is to be repeated, there is no need to repeat mistakes.

This is one meeting where I strongly recommend the taking of minutes. They should be distributed to all who participate and should become part of the planning for the following year. If you are repeating the event, it's never too early to get to work on it.

I do hope I've given you a lot to think about. There is no

(*Opposite*) *Old-fashioned fire equipment can be a colorful addition to a parade.*

formula for the perfect parade, but I do hope you find a path to take your event close as possible. Making people happy is a very special experience. It's even more special when you can share it with others—and that's what a parade is all about.

As they say on opening night, break a leg!

Santa's Thanksgiving Parade helpers in Detroit put the finishing touches on the 15½ foot papier mâché head of Gepetto, created as part of the Detroit Renaissance Foundation gift for the children of Detroit.

Appendix

GENERAL PARADE REGULATIONS
ATLANTA DOGWOOD FESTIVAL PARADE

1. No individual or unit will be allowed to take part in the parade without the prior approval of the Parade Committee.

2. All individuals and organizations participating in the parade are subject, while in the City of Atlanta, to the laws and regulations of that jurisdiction. Failure to adhere to those laws and regulations, or to obey the lawful command of an official empowered to give such command, will be cause for immediate removal from the parade and may be cause for arrest and/or fine.

3. The conduct and movement of the parade will be controlled by Marshals assigned for that purpose. Participants will obey the directions of the Marshals as they relate to the parade. Failure to do so will cause the offending individual or unit to be removed from the parade.

4. All units must be identified so that spectators and television cameras can easily see the name of each unit or its sponsor. Identification on floats must be on both sides, running the entire length of the float or twenty feet, whichever is the lesser. Marching units and others must be preceded by marchers carrying banners or signs which can be easily read at a distance of 100 feet. All identification signs and banners must be carried and/or displayed in such a way as to assure they can be read even in rain or high wind. Young children should not be assigned to carry identification banners.

5. Units may contain no element higher than 13 feet, to provide clearance of overhead wires and traffic lights.

6. The parade will move at the rate of 120 adult steps to the minute. No unit incapable of maintaining that pace for the duration of the parade will be included.

7. All units with children under third-grade level will be expected to station persons along the parade route to assist tired marchers. Alternative uniforms or costumes should be available in case of cold or rainy weather.

8. Throwing of any object from the parade will not be allowed. No firecrackers or discharge of firearms will be allowed.

9. The Dogwood Festival maintains a policy of public liability insurance to protect against any claims by spectators against the Festival. Parade participants should ask their own insurance agents if their insurance offers them sufficient protection while their units are in the parade.

10. Floats rented or purchased through the Parade Committee will be constructed and operated as provided by the regulations and codes of the City of Atlanta. Participants who provide their own floats are responsible for adherence to these regulations and codes and should familiarize themselves with them.

11. Individuals and organizations in the parade are expected to perform courteously, in good taste, and with safety in mind at all times during the formation, execution, and dismissal of the parade. Marshals will remove any person or unit that in their sole discretion violates this regulation.

APPLICATION TO ENTER UNIT IN THE
DOGWOOD FESTIVAL PARADE

The organization named herein requests consideration as a participant in the Atlanta Dogwood Festival Parade. The undersigned warrants that he/she is empowered to sign for the applying organization and that he/she has read and understands the provisions set forth in the "General Parade Regulations" section of the instructions received with this application form.

SPONSORING ORGANIZATION
Name of organization: _St. Rosalie's Knights of Columbus_
Type of organization: (commercial, religious, charitable, educational, scientific, literary, or other) _religious_

Address: _1365 13th Avenue_
Brooklyn, New York 11265

Phone: _(212) 232-8100_
Contact person assigned to work with Dogwood Festival Parade Committee:
Name: _Joseph Beneduccio_ Position: _Grand Knight_
Home address: _1778 71st Street_
Brooklyn, New York 11228

Home phone: _(212) 256-3068_

APPLICATION SUBMITTED BY:

_1/21/82_ _Father Michael Venutto_ _Program_
Date   Signature   _Administrator_
                                     Title:

The Atlanta Dogwood Festival application is representative of forms used by many parade organizations.

151

BAND APPLICATION FORM

PLEASE TYPE OR PRINT

1. Name of organization or school _Bayberry Sr. High School_
2. Mailing address _1501 Bayberry Road, Boston, Mass. 06617_
3. Telephone number (area code) _1(617) 719-9870_
4. Name of musical unit _Bayberry Marching Lions_
5. Name of director _Mr. Andrew Barnes_
6. Address of director _1641-74th Avenue Boston, Mass. 06617_
7. Name of principal or administrator _Mark R. Siegal_
8. A letter from your school principal or administrator indicating approval of your band's participation <u>must</u> be attached to this application.
9. Number in Band (include all personnel)

Color Guard	_12_	Special Groups	_10 Rifles_
Drum Majors	_3_	Other Groups	_—_
Twirlers	_15_	Band Players	_96_

   Total Number of Personnel in Band _136_

10. Age span of members: _13_ to _17_
11. Complete description of above groups. (Please be as detailed as possible. This information will be used for publicity releases and for national television script. If additional space is required, attach additional sheets.)

    Rifle/Color Guard – girls and boys: White slacks,
    royal blue tabards trimmed in gold. Drum majors/
    players: white slacks, royal blue jackets trimmed
    with gold braid. Drum majors have gold overlay.
    Twirlers: white boots, ruffled blouses, gold vests
    and satin (short) skirts.

12. Description of Band Uniforms (color, style, etc.) _See 11._

13. Number of ranks _16_ and files _12_ in the block band. The total estimated marching length of the band and auxiliary units and twirlers is _150_ feet.

14. Record of events band has participated in, honors won, etc. _National Cherry Blossom Festival, 1980; International Youth and Music Festival, Vienna, Austria, 1981_

152

15. Media contacts to whom publicity releases should be sent if you are selected. (List in order of preference, as it may not be possible to send releases to all.)

    NEWSPAPER-RADIO-TV   ADDRESS

16. Transportation: Special arrangements are made for parking buses and trucks in the parade area; therefore, it is necessary that the following information be furnished:

    Number of buses used to transport band ___6___

    Number of trucks used to transport instruments and/or equipment ___2___

    NOTE: Because of limited parking space in the parade marshalling area, no space can be provided for parking automobiles.

17. A brochure containing the following must accompany this application:

    a. Pictures of your marching band
    b. Pictures of the band's auxiliary units (twirlers, majorettes, etc.)
    c. Any newspaper/magazine articles covering your band's activities
    d. Copies of concert programs

18. MAIL APPLICATION TO: (name and address of your organization)

    The Selection Committee will evaluate bands for selection between November 1 and December 31. Please return this application form by October 31.

    Please note: We cannot underwrite any of a participating unit's expenses, so plan accordingly. Evidence of public liability insurance covering activities of your band and the acts of individual members as well as sponsoring organizations must be attached to this application.

153

SPECIAL UNIT APPLICATION FORM

PLEASE TYPE OR PRINT

1. NAME OF PARTICIPATING UNIT _Fort Lee Junior Equestrians_
2. UNIT MAILING ADDRESS _2107 Bridge Ave Fort Lee, N.J. 06837_
   Street   City   State   Zip

3. TELEPHONE NUMBER: (AREA CODE) _(201) 648-7313_
4. NAME OF DIRECTOR/LEADER _Mrs. Janet Lewis_
5. If your unit is a part of or is sponsored by an organization, a letter
   from your organization or unit administrator indicating approval of
   your unit's participation must be attached to this application.
   Evidence of public liability insurance covering activities of your
   unit and the acts of individual members as well as sponsoring organizations must be attached to your application.

6. NUMBER IN UNIT _10_ EQUIPMENT _____ PERSONNEL _25_ ANIMALS _10_
7. COMPLETE DESCRIPTION OF UNIT (Describe personnel, equipment, animals, etc. Include color, style, etc. This information will be used
   for publicity releases and for national television script. If
   additional space is required, attach a supplementary sheet.)
   Group is made up of boys and girls and 8-13
   who are the finest riders in the Northern New
   Jersey area. All are outfitted in English style
   riding garb.

8. MARCHING DATA: Length of Unit: _40_ Feet   Marching Width: _15_ Feet
9. RECORDS OF UNIT (Events unit has participated in, honors won, etc.)
   1st place - North American Championships, N.Y., 1980
   Blue Ribbon Group - President's Race, Washington D.C. 1981
   Queen's Choice - 1981 Cherry Blossom Festival

10. Media contacts to whom publicity releases should be sent if you
    are selected. Please list them in order of preference as it may not
    be possible to send releases to all.
    If you have a personal contact to whom the release should be sent,
    please give name.
    NEWSPAPER-RADIO-TV   ADDRESS

154

11. TRANSPORTATION: Special arrangements are.made for parking of the buses or trucks in the parade area; therefore, we ask you to complete the following:

Number of buses used to transport your unit _1_

Number of trucks used to transport your equipment _5_

NOTE: Because of limited parking space in marshalling area, no space can be provided for parking automobiles.

12. A brochure containing the following information must accompany this form:

   a. Pictures of your unit and equipment

   b. Newspaper/magazine clippings covering your unit's activities

   c. Other information that will help the parade committee evaluate your unit

NOTE: All materials will be returned to you on or about June 15th.

MAIL APPLICATION AND RELATED MATERIAL TO: (name and address of your organization)

The Selection Committee will start evaluation on or about November 1st. This application form should be returned at your earliest convenience.

Please note: We cannot underwrite any of a participating unit's expenses and your plans should be made accordingly.

155

APPLICATION OF PAPIER-MACHÉ TO CHICKEN WIRE FORMS.

MATERIALS:

PAIL,

PASTE BRUSH,

WHEAT PASTE,

WRAPPING PAPER,

PASTING BOARD.

PAPER. Many different grades of paper can be used, but the one more readily available in most places and the best for the inexperienced to use, is common brown wrapping paper. This paper is available in different thicknesses such as 30 lb., 60 lb. and 90 lb. weights. For the normal covering of a chicken wire form for floats, 2 coats of paper should be applied; the base coat or first layer should be of the heavier weight, such as 60 lb. or 90 lb., and the second or finish coat of the lighter 30 lb. paper. Additional layers of paper may be applied depending on the strength and smoothness desired.

PASTE. Use a good grade of Wheat Paste, such as that used for wallpaper.

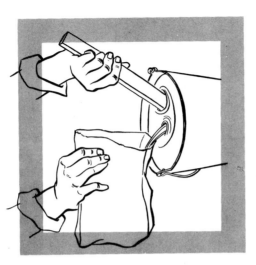

1. Mix paste thoroughly to a thick creamy consistency. Mix only a small portion of paste to start with until you become more familiar with the quantities of paste required to do the work.

2. Cut or tear the wrapping paper into pieces approximately 1 ft. square. (Torn edges on paper will make smoother joints when pasted than sharp cut edges.)

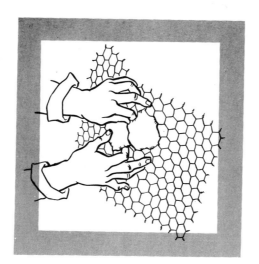

3. Place the first piece of paper on a pasting board (pasting board may be a scrap piece of wallboard, boxboard, plywood, etc.). Brush a liberal quantity of paste over the entire sheet of paper, place the next sheet of paper on top of the first piece and apply paste in the same manner. Repeat this process until you have a stack of about 10 pieces piled up, many more pieces may be pasted in a stack, but this should be ample for a start. (If paper in stack tends to get too dry as you are using it, apply more wet paste to top pieces as you peel them off.) The paper is now ready to apply to the chicken wire form.

4. Peel off the top piece of wet pasted paper. Tear off small pieces about 3 or 4 inches square; place them on the chicken wire form, and hook the edges under the wire. These pieces are known as "ties," and when the paper is dry they will hold securely to the wire form. Place these "ties" several inches apart around the immediate working area.

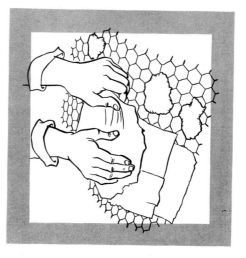

5. Apply larger pieces of paper (about 6" square) over the wire form where the "ties" have been put. Overlap each succeeding piece (much the way shingles are applied on a roof), and at intervals hook the corners of the pieces under the wire for additional "ties."

Repeat this procedure until the form is completely covered with the first layer of paper. Allow this layer to dry. When you are ready to apply the second coat, brush a liberal amount of wet paste over the first layer; the second coat is then applied in the same method as the first, with the exception of the ties which are not required. When the wet pasted paper dries it will shrink and draw very tightly on the form it has been applied to, so the following points should be kept in mind: A large piece of paper will shrink and draw much more than several smaller pieces, which allow more slip at the overlaps, and are easier to form over compound surfaces. Large pieces may be used on big mass areas, but on objects with detailed surfaces or a shape such as a ball, where the paper coat completely encloses the form, much smaller pieces should be used so that the shrinking paper does not tend to crush the form when it dries.

From Vaughn's Parade and Float Guide, by L. F. Vaughn (T.S. Denison and Company, Minneapolis). Copyright © 1956. Used by permission.

Index